The army, politics and
society in Germany, 1933–45

Klaus-Jürgen Müller

The army, politics and society in Germany 1933–45

Studies in the army's relation to Nazism

St. Martin's Press   New York

Armee, Politik und Gesellschaft in Deutschland 1933–45 copyright ©
Verlag Ferdinand Schöningh KG, Jühenplatz 1,
D–4790 Paderborn, West Germany

This translation copyright © Manchester University Press 1987

First published in the United States of America in 1987

Printed in Great Britain

ISBN 0-312-00918-6

Library of Congress Cataloging in Publication Data applied for

Contents

Preface

The role of the armed forces under the system of National Socialism has long been a central theme of political as well as historical debate over the phenomenon of the Hitler regime and its development; almost, in fact, since the very beginning of the Third Reich. The question was first examined in detail and on the basis of extensive source material in my book *Das Heer und Hitler*, which covered the period from 1933 to 1940, and in Manfred Messerschmidt's *Die Wehrmacht im NS-Staat* for the period up to 1945.[1] In these studies a first attempt was made to set the problem of the relation between the army and the Nazi regime in a historical perspective. The historical treatment of this problem, which had hitherto been predominantly moral and political in emphasis, was able to draw for essential elements of its interpretive framework on those works which had laid the foundations of the problem of continuity in German history, in particular those of Fritz Fischer[2] and Andreas Hillgruber,[3] which analysed Germany's politics as a great power from Bismarck to Hitler.

In the meantime the debate about the structure of the Nazi regime, a debate which far from being closed is not yet even approaching consensus, has furnished new insights relevant to the theme of this book. Also significant for the illumination it provides of the army's role in the National Socialist system has been the re-examination of topics such as rearmament and the economy, and the influence of industrialisation and technological development on the military. In particular, the first results of the detailed study of the military and rearmament policies of the general staff between the wars are now available. The enlargement and improvement of our knowledge, together with the recent recognition of the importance of particular factors, have put the attempt to situate the interpretation of relations between the armed forces and the Nazi power structure within a comprehensive historical perspective on a much sounder basis.

The first of the three studies – each complete in itself – presented here attempts just such an historical treatment of the problem. It contributes to a preliminary re-evaluation of the army's role in the National Socialist State in the following way: two crucial elements of recent German history, the political tradition of the Prusso-German military elite and the phenomenon of 'total warfare' involving the whole of society are placed in a descriptive and interpretative context and the problem is subjected to multidimensional treatment.

The developments which led the German military elite from the Garrison Church, where in 1933 it had gathered around Hindenburg and Hitler, to Karlhorst, where in 1945 one of Hitler's field-marshals had to sign the declaration of surrender, were determined neither by the feudalism of the Junkers nor by the 'industrialisation and socialisation' of modern warfare alone. These two factors – more specifically the claim to political leadership derived from the Prusso-German tradition *and* the nature of modern warfare between industrial states, warfare which involved the whole of society — must be taken together. They will be shown to have determined in a decisive way the attitude of the military elite and its reaction to the principal challenges that arose from socio-economic change and political upheaval – challenges to which, in the end, it was not equal.

The confrontation of the army and National Socialism which is here to be situated in a historical framework was characterised by reactions of both *co-operation* and *opposition*. The specific nature and development of these two reactions are more precisely defined and explained in the two following chapters.

A concrete study is offered of the political thought and professional conduct of the Chief of the General Staff, Ludwig Beck, by his office and by personality one of the most prominent representatives of the military elite. As a co-founder of the new army in the Third Reich and later as a leading figure in the national conservative opposition to Hitler he exemplifies the development from co-operation to opposition in a particularly striking way. The possibilities and the bounds of the activities of high-ranking military officers in the Nazi state are given clearer definition as a function of tradition, of a view of the world coloured by individual experience, and of political and military-political conditions which they themselves had helped to create.

The third study sketches a descriptive and explanatory framework, attempting to take analysis of the historical phenomenon of German military opposition beyond the level of moral and political debate which has so far predominated so as to make possible more comprehensive historical interpretation.

All three studies are revised and expanded versions of lectures given at universities in England (London, Oxford, Cambridge, York, Lancaster and Manchester), America (Ann Arbor) and Canada (McGill/Montreal) and presented to the thirty-second Deutschen Historikertag* in Hamburg.

I thank therefore, above all, those colleagues and students who have, by their criticism on those occasions, helped me to see the problems and issues more clearly and to re-examine my own views. Special thanks are due to my friends and colleagues, Michael Geyer (Ann Arbor) and Wilhelm Deist (Freiburg-im-Breisgau) for a long-standing and stimulating exchange of ideas on the problems treated here.

Hamburg, 15 May 1979   Klaus-Jürgen Müller

Notes

1 Manfred Messerschmidt, *Die Wehrmacht im NS-Staat. Zeit der Indoktrination*, Hamburg, 1969 (Truppe und Verwaltung, 16); Klaus-Jürgen Müller, *Das Heer und Hitler. Armee und nationalsozialistisches Regime 1933–1940*, Stuttgart, 1969 (Beiträge zur Militär- und Kriegsgeschichte, 10).

2 Fischer's interpretation, which he has expanded further since his *Griff nach der Weltmacht* (Düsseldorf, 1971) most recently meaningfully summarised in the published account of his notable paper at the Hamburg historians' conference: Fritz Fischer, *Bündnis der Eliten. Zur Kontinuität der Machtstrukturen in Deutschland 1871–1945*, Düsseldorf, 1979.

3 Especially Andreas Hillgruber, *Grossmachtpolitik und Militarismus im 20. Jahrhundert*, Beiträge zum Kontinuitätsproblem, Düsseldorf, 1974.

4 cf. Michael Geyer, 'Aufrüstung oder Sicherheit. Reichswehr und die Krise der Machtpolitik 1924–1936', thesis, Freiburg, 1976 (published under the same title, Wiesbaden, 1980); Wilhelm Deist, 'Das militärische Instrument für den Krieg', in Militärgeschichtliches For-

schungsamt (ed.), *Das Deutsche Reich und der Zweite Weltkrieg, I, Ursachen und Voraussetzungen*, Stuttgart, 1979; *id.*, 'Zum Problem der deutschen Aufrüstung', *Francia*, 5 (1977), pp. 539–65, and *id.*, 'Heeresausrüstung und Aggression 1936–1939' (paper given at the Franco-German Historians' Colloquium, Bonn, 1978), later published in the supplement to *Francia*, as well as Klaus-Jürgen Müller, *General Ludwig Beck. Studien und Dokumente zur politischen Vorstellungswelt und beruflichen Tätigkeit des Generalstabschefs 1933–1938*, Boppard, 1979.

For Inge

Introduction

by William Carr *University of Sheffield*

Since the collapse of the Third Reich in the spring of 1945 an immense literature has poured forth on virtually every aspect of Hitler's Germany: political, social and economic. No aspect has aroused more controversy or aroused greater general interest than the part played by the German officer corps in the *Machtergreifung* in January 1933 and in maintaining Hitler in power thereafter. Over the years interpretations have oscillated between wholesale condemnation of the officer corps, whose members were generally depicted in wartime propaganda as tight-lipped martinets complete with duelling scars and monocle and, on the other hand, a conviction that the overwhelming majority of German officers were decent fellows who did no more than their bounden duty to their country and in so doing upheld the highest traditions of the officer corps.

In 1945 the victorious allied powers had no doubt that the officer corps, or at least its most influential representatives, had been the willing accomplices of the Nazis. Wartime propagandists had slotted Hitler into the mainstream of German history as the natural successor to Frederick the Great, Bismarck and William II, the latest in a line of Prussian militarists bent on world domination. And, more important, in the months preceding the trial at Nuremberg of the major war criminals investigating teams had gathered together an impressive mass of documentation on the basis of which the German General Staff and the High Command were charged under the indictment as criminal organisations. Although the tribunal rejected this allegation on purely technical grounds, Lord Justice Lawrence, delivering the verdict of the tribunal, was forthright in his condemnation of the General Staff and the High Command.

They have been responsible in large measure for the miseries and suffering that have fallen on millions of men, women and children. They have been a disgrace to the honourable profession of arms. Without their military guidance the aggressive ambitions of Hitler and his fellow Nazis would have been academic and sterile . . . they were certainly a ruthless military caste. The contemporary German militarism flourished briefly with its recent ally, National Socialism, as well as, or better than, it had in the generations of the past. Many of these men have made a mockery of their soldier's oath of obedience to military orders. When it suits their defence they say that they had to obey; when confronted with Hitler's brutal crimes, which have been shown to have been within their general knowledge, they say they disobeyed. The truth is that they actively participated in all these crimes, or sat silent and acquiescent witnessing the commission of crime on a scale larger and more shocking than the world has ever had the misfortune to know.[1]

The two soldiers among the twelve accused — Wilhelm Keitel, chief of Army High Command, and Alfred Jodl, chief of operations at High Command – were both found guilty and condemned to death on all four counts of conspiracy, crimes against peace, war crimes and crimes against humanity.

Historians were not untouched by the wave of moral indignation sweeping through a world profoundly shocked by incontrovertible evidence of large-scale genocide practised on the Jews with cold-blooded deliberation by the Nazis. In *The Nemesis of Power: the German Army in Politics, 1918–1945*, published in 1953, Sir John Wheeler-Bennett, a gifted amateur historian, was scathing in his condemnation of Germany's military elite for their behind-the-scenes role in helping put Hitler in power and keeping him there. Though he recognised that the military figures implicated in the 1944 bomb plot to kill Hitler were moved by considerations of honour, Wheeler-Bennett was relieved that its failure had removed the need for the allied powers to negotiate a peace with reactionary Prussian officers; unconditional surrender and the complete destruction of German military power were a much more desirable outcome.

German historians, having survived Nazi tyranny only to emerge into a cold and unfriendly post-war world, were reluctant to acquiesce in the superficial blanket condemnations of the German people then in vogue, a classic example of which was Alan Taylor's *The Course of German History: a Survey of the Development of German History since 1815*. German historians such as Friedrich Meinecke, Hans Herzfeld and Gerhard Ritter, whilst in no way

Introduction 3

condoning the crimes of the regime, sought to place fascism in a
European framework; unlike Marxist historians in Eastern Europe,
they blamed its excesses not on the machinations of finance
capitalism but on the totalitarian tendencies allegedly implicit in
mass democracy from the time of the Jacobins onward and on the
disintegrating effects of modern technology on the established
social order – both favourite themes in High Tory circles in these
years, with social revolution on the march in large parts of the
continent. Germany's military leaders emerged from this
reappraisal as no longer stereotyped reactionaries directly
responsible for much of what had happened in Germany in the
1930s and 1940s but rather as short-sighted and hidebound
individuals completely out of their depth in the hard world of
politics and all too easily swept off their (on the whole honourable)
feet by the demoniacal power of Hitler. This was much the line
taken by Lord Bullock in a masterly biography of the Führer:
Hitler: a Study in Tyranny (1951), which has still not been
surpassed in its class, and also by Gordon Craig in *The Politics of
the Prussian Army, 1640–1945* in 1955.

In the course of the 1950s the image of the German military
changed even more. At the end of the war the allied powers in their
determination to prevent another outburst of German aggression
resolved never to put arms into the hands of Germans again.
However, in the early 1950s mounting fear of Russia persuaded the
American and British (and more reluctantly the French) govern-
ments that German rearmament was a military necessity and the
lesser of two evils. Despite misgivings in the Western world that
rearmament would effectively terminate all hope of the re-
unification of the two Germanies, the Federal Republic was
admitted to NATO in 1955. A German army, the Bundeswehr, was
formed initially with 150,000 volunteers but a year later conscription was reintroduced to increase it to 500,000 men. Its new
leaders, faced with the delicate task of creating an *esprit de corps*
for the new army in keeping with the democratic *mores* of the new
republic, had to come to terms with the record of the old
Wehrmacht and the Nuremberg judgement of 1946. The rehabilit-
ation of the old officer corps was assisted materially by the
publication of several memoirs by high-ranking generals in which
their authors attempted in varying degrees to exonerate the
Wehrmacht from responsibility for the Nazi crimes. In the deceased

Führer ex-Wehrmacht generals found the perfect scapegoat, a fanatic whom they had (allegedly) despised and whose crazy racialism could be blamed for the disastrous attack on the Soviet Union (about which they had, in fact, enthused). In the days before structural history cast some doubt on the assumption that the 'great men of history' determined the course of events virtually unaided, it was deceptively easy to lay all responsibility for unpleasantness on a power-mad dictator with Germany in his grip and manipulating the German people hither and thither at will.

One slight problem remained: the conspirators of 1944 could not be written off as traitors even though they had broken their personal oath of allegiance to Hitler as Supreme Commander of the Wehrmacht — not an example which even the most democratically-minded commanding generals want to see their officers emulate. An uneasy compromise was arrived at. The men of 1944 were recognised as honourable soldiers acting as they did because, by virtue of being in the corridors of power, they had gained special insight into the criminal nature of the regime. The rest of the officer corps, lacking these insights and simply obeying orders, could be exonerated from all blame and indeed be looked up to as men of honour who fought loyally to the bitter end.

The new orthodoxy rubbed off on to historians such as Harold J. Gordon. In a persuasively argued book, *The Reichswehr and the German Republic, 1919–1926* (1957), he zealously defended the record of the Reichswehr and of its founder, General Hans von Seeckt, and rejected — rightly — the moralistic assumption of British and American historians that there was a specifically German strain of militarism which had exerted a baneful influence on the course of German history since the days of Frederick William I of Prussia, the 'Sergeant King'. That the Reichswehr was never integrated into the republic it was supposed to serve he attributed not to Seeckt's notoriously anti-republican ethos (which Gordon glossed over) but much more to the hostility of left-wing parties to all armies. Finally, he rejected invidious comparisons between British, American and German traditions; was it not obvious that a country with uncertain frontiers, hostile neighbours and inadequate defences — all questionable assumptions — was bound to take a more pessimistic view of the future than the Anglo-Saxons? Sympathy for the Reichswehr was also evident in Robert O'Neill's *The German Army and the Nazi Party, 1933–39*

(1966), which confirmed the view of Bullock and Craig that the majority of officers were 'like rudderless ships amidst swift currents', taken in by and eventually taken over by the Nazis they despised at heart.[3]

This interpretation was irretrievably shattered in the course of the 1960s. For this several developments were responsible. In the first place the archives, seized by the Americans in 1945 and transported to Alexandria, Virginia, were returned to the Federal Republic, enabling a generation of young German historians, for whom the war was, in many cases, no more than a childhood memory, to begin serious research into all aspects of the Third Reich. Secondly, Fritz Fischer's pioneering work, *Griff nach der Weltmacht. Die Kriegszielpolitik des kaiserlichen Deutschlands 1914–1918*, published in 1961, gave a decisive twist to the direction taken by this research. Whereas the older generation of German historians likened the Nazi period to a *Betriebsunfall* or industrial accident, an aberration from the liberal traditions of Weimar – to which the Federal Republic had now returned with relief – Fischer made himself thoroughly unpopular with his colleagues (in the initial stages) by emphasising the element of continuity between the aims and objectives of Hitler's Germany and those of Bismarck and William II. This theme has remained in the forefront of research ever since and has been elaborated upon by several scholars, especially Andreas Hillgruber. In *Deutschlands Rolle in der Vorgeschichte der beiden Weltkriege* (1967) and *Kontinuität und Diskontinuität in der deutschen Aussenpolitik von Bismarck bis Hitler* (1969) the Cologne historian examined the causes of the two world wars and identified a link between them in the *Ostpolitik* of General Erich Ludendorff, his advocacy of wholesale annexation of territory in Eastern Europe at the expense of Russia adumbrating the policy Hitler was to follow.

Thirdly, Fischer laid what for a German historian was unusual emphasis on the social and economic forces which moulded the shape of politics in William II's Germany. Simultaneously the important renaissance of Marxist studies occurring in the Federal Republic in this decade also focused attention on these factors in the historical equation. Consequently structural history came into fashion, i.e. the emphasis in historical studies shifted away from purely political history and away from the obsessive interest in the personality of Adolf Hitler – hitherto a dominant theme in much of the writing on the Third Reich – and towards an investigation of the social, economic and cultural determinants of political action. Much useful work has been done since then unravelling the structures of Nazi Germany and demonstrating that in some respects it was a much less monolithic society than generally supposed. Applied to the army, once research moved beyond a narrow preoccupation with the political relations between the military leaders and Hitler and tried to anchor the army in the broader setting of domestic policy, it quickly became apparent that the favourable verdict of the 1950s could not be upheld.

Already in 1964, before the new fashion took root, Francis Carsten, an émigré from Nazi Germany who had established his reputation with pioneering studies of the origins of Prussia and of the German Estates in the early modern period, set the critical tone of the next two decades with *Reichswehr und Politik 1918–1933*. This well researched book, like Gordon's essentially a piece of political history, sharply criticised the army's role in the Weimar Republic. Some of the myths growing up around Seeckt and General Wilhelm Groener, Minister of Defence from 1928 to 1932, were dispelled. And, although Carsten conceded that army command had not been directly responsible for Hitler's appointment as Chancellor, nevertheless the general conclusion of the author was that by its 'stony silence' towards the republic the Reichswehr had contributed materially to its collapse.

By the end of the decade substantial works by German historians on the period after 1933 had confirmed Carsten's negative picture of the army's role. In his first book, *Das Heer und Hitler. Armee und nationalsozialistisches Regime 1933–1940*, published in 1969, Klaus-Jürgen Müller examined army opposition to Hitler between 1933 and 1940, and for the first time a historian dared to look closely and critically at the record of General Ludwig Beck, a soldier widely revered as the epitome of 'the other Germany' and the heart and soul of the military opposition to Hitler. In the same year Manfred Messerschmidt's *Die Wehrmacht im NS Staat. Zeit der Indoktrination* demonstrated beyond all doubt that co-operation between army and regime was much closer than had been generally supposed. Serious doubt was cast at last on the distinction usually drawn by historians between the great majority of army officers (of whom General Freiherr Werner von Fritsch, commander-in-chief of the army from 1934 to 1938, was the prototype) who were supposed to have looked down their aristocratic noses at the Nazis and held them at bay as much as possible, and on the other hand soldiers such as Keitel, Jodl and General Walther von Brauchitsch, commander-in-chief of the army from 1938 to 1941, who allegedly were to blame for opening the floodgates to Nazi infiltration of the army. There was, in fact, continuity between the aims of Fritsch and Brauchitsch; both agreed with the Nazis on the need for rearmament and for the mobilisation of the people for war, and co-operated with the regime to a greater or lesser extent on that basis.

Co-operation between the army and the Nazis extended further than that, as investigation of German policy in occupied Europe has shown. In 1978 Christian Streit's *Keine Kameraden. Die Wehrmacht und die sowjetischen Kriegsgefangenen 1941–1945* appeared. This detailed analysis of the treatment of Russian prisoners of war, 58% of whom died in German captivity, destroyed the myth repeated, for example, in Joachim Fest's best-seller *Hitler* (1973; translated into English 1974) that the army busied itself exclusively with fighting in Russia and left the murder of Jews and communists to the *Einsatzgruppen* or murder squads of police and SS operating in rear echelon. The truth, established long ago at the Nuremberg trials but conveniently forgotten by powerful circles in the Federal Republic, was that the army and SS worked hand-in-glove during the Russian campaign, conducting a 'war of racial annihilation' against 'sub-humans' against which very few officers seem to have protested. Before the attack on Russia, detailed arrangements were made at top-level discussions to prevent any repetition of the (limited) army protests about the employment of *Einsatzgruppen* in Poland. Not content with shifting the responsibility on to the murder squads, the army co-operated actively at all levels first in the shooting of communist commissars and Jews and later in the exploitation of Russian POWs as slave labour in Germany. Moreover the bestial treatment of these prisoners did, in Streit's opinion, prepare the way for the systematic murder of European Jewry from the autumn of 1941 onwards. So Streit concludes that the deeds of the Nazis would have been 'unthinkable without extensive and willing co-operation from a large part of the German ruling class'.[4] One may legitimately argue about the degree and extent of ruling-class involvement in Nazi war crimes, but one thing is certain: Streit's

careful documentation of old truths leaves no doubt that the army
did not 'keep its uniform clean'.

Streit's thesis was confirmed in 1981 by the authoritative work
on the murder squads published after twenty years of research by
the prestigious Institut für Zeitgeschichte in Munich: *Die Truppe
des Weltanschauungskrieges. Die Einsatzgruppen der Sicherheitspolizei und des SD 1938–1942.* The authors, Helmut Krausnick, a
former director of the Institute, and Hans-Heinrich Wilhelm, show
that even in Poland, where it has been usual in the past to remember
only the protests of a few officers, the army was in fact deeply
involved in criminal activities. Similarly in Russia; for example, the
notorious massacre of 33,771 Kiev Jews in the Babi Yar ravine,
described so vividly by Donald Michael Thomas in *The White
Hotel*, was organised by an *Einsatzgruppe* in conjunction with the
town commandant of Kiev and 29 Corps of the Sixth Army. There
is massive evidence, too, that high-ranking officers such as Field
Marshal Walther von Reichenau, General Erich von Manstein and
General Hermann Hoth approved criminal activities of this kind.
The authors conclude not unreasonably that without the co-
operation of the Wehrmacht the regime could hardly have
succeeded in its murderous plans.[5]

As a knowledge of German is still a relatively rare accomplish-
ment in English-speaking countries, the findings of recent research
on the German army are not as widely known as they ought to be.
The translation of K. J. Müller's second book, *Armee, Politik und
Gesellschaft in Deutschland 1933–1945*, which first appeared in
1979, is therefore greatly to be welcomed. In three self-contained
essays Müller succeeds remarkably well in synthesising much of
the latest research and at the same time offers the reader a more
convincing explanation of relations between army and state than
we have had in the past. The great merit of his approach, it seems to
me, is that while not in any way denying the validity of moral
imperatives to drive men to action – or not, as the case may be – he
does attempt to delineate the broad structural parameters without
which valid historical judgements on men or on institutions cannot
be made.

Two structural factors which helped form the outlook of the
officer corps between 1918 and 1945 were, in his view: firstly, the
Prussian military tradition, and secondly, the technological revolution of modern times which has completely transformed the nature

of warfare, destroying the old professional elitism of the officer corps. On Prussia's military traditions much has been written, notably by Gerhard Ritter in the four-volume *Staatskunst und Kriegshandwerk*, published in 1959 and translated as *The Sword and the Scepter: the Problem of Militarism in Germany*, which traces the history of militarism from Frederick the Great's onslaught on Silesia in 1740 to the armistice of 1918.

For the second theme Müller relies heavily on the pioneering work of Michael Geyer: *Aufrüstung oder Sicherheit. Die Reichswehr und die Krise der Machtpolitik 1924–1936*, a Freiburg dissertation published in 1980. Geyer attempts to anchor rearmament and military strategy firmly in a socio-historical context. His thesis is that modern states have a choice between rearmament or security, as the title suggests, because the industrialisation of war had endangered society; the destructive power of modern weaponry has undermined the military professionalism on which the security of states traditionally rested; in the past soldiers employed their expertise to help achieve limited foreign political objectives whilst containing inevitable losses within reasonable bounds. Technological advance however, revolutionised war, making its outcome – at least in the pre-nuclear age – dependent upon the fullest possible exploitation of a state's resources in manpower and raw materials, ushering in the total war situation of the twentieth century when all become soldiers. Applied to Germany, this meant that her only hope of successfully revising the Treaty of Versailles in the inter-war years – the objective the army was committed to from the outset – without in the process destroying Germany was to devise a political concept holding foreign policy, economy and military strategy together in a delicate, ever changing balance of forces. This was attempted only once, fleetingly, by General Groener, who was, however, removed from office in 1932. Instead of a balanced strategy the army opted for total mobilisation of Germany's resources and, ignoring diplomatic and political restraints, relied solely on military power to serve its political ends. The accelerating pace of rearmament in 1935–36 – for which the army was more responsible than Hitler (which is not to say he did not welcome it) – so alarmed the other powers that they commenced their own rearmament and so trapped Germany in an arms race she could not win.

Geyer's influence can be seen at work in the first volume of *Das Deutsche Reich und der Zweite Weltkrieg* (1979), an ambitious

ten-volume work on the second world war intended for a general
audience and written by historians at the Militärgeschichtliches
Forschungsamt in Freiburg. Wilhelm Deist's important essay on
rearmament demonstrates very clearly its central importance for
both foreign and domestic policy in the mid-1930s.[6] Incidentally,
this volume as a whole, with impressive contributions from Manfred Messerschmidt, Hans-Erich Volkmann and Wolfram Wette,
represents a notable and welcome victory for structural historians
over the narrowly traditional approach of the military historian.

A few comments on Müller's essays themselves. The first offers
an exciting new perspective for understanding the role of the army
in the Third Reich. Müller argues persuasively that after 1918 the
army was fighting a rearguard action on two fronts: first, to
maintain that privileged position vis-à-vis the state which it
enjoyed in William II's Germany; and, secondly, to preserve its
professionalism when the concept of total war was steadily eroding
the old dualism between the military and the civilian government.
As long as the army could keep its privileged political status – as it
did in the Weimar Republic – it could preserve its professionalism.
Hitler's clever play with the so-called 'two pillars theory' confirmed
(temporarily only) the entente between army and state and was a
sufficient reason why the army looked on complaisantly while the
Nazis with characteristic brutality crushed all opposition to the
regime. Müller rightly sees 1938 as a turning-point when changes
in command personnel put Hitler in effective charge of the army
and ended its pretensions to be the equal partner of the state.
Subsequently officers were reduced to the status of functionaries
content with their professional duties narrowly defined, a position
perfectly acceptable to the vast majority. A minority, of whom
General Ludwig Beck became the most celebrated figure, resented
this loss of status and started to oppose the regime, fighting for the
restoration of the lost world of imperial Germany where 'red
stripes' formed a political and social elite able to exert influence
over the whole field of policy.

On Beck, the subject of the second essay, Müller is an established expert. In 1980 he published a pioneering study, *General
Ludwig Beck. Studien und Dokumente zur politischen-
militärischen Vorstellungswelt und Tätigkeit des Generalstabchefs
des deutschen Heeres 1933–1938* in which he rejected the stereotyped picture of Beck so popular in military circles and given a

new lease of life by the Canadian historian Peter Hoffmann in *Widerstand Staatsstreich und Attentat. Probleme des Umsturzes* in 1969. Hoffman still clings to the old view of Beck as a man of tender conscience who very early on understood the perfidious nature of the regime, resigned in 1938 – profoundly shocked by the impending attack on Czechoslovakia – and planned to overthrow Hitler, continued to oppose him during the war and perished in the aftermath of the 1944 bomb plot, a record which won him a reputation as the very personification of 'the other Germany' and the heart and soul of the military resistance to Hitler.

Müller is rightly critical of the tendency to read history backwards and assume a continuum in Beck's behaviour which the documentary evidence does not confirm. The fact is that Beck was at first an enthusiastic supporter of Hitler, anxious to press ahead with the creation of an offensive army to be used either for military action or as a weapon of diplomatic coercion to regain for Germany her dominant position in Europe, which required the subjection of Austria and Czechoslovakia. What conflicts did arise to trouble this relationship are attributable not to a root-and-branch aversion to Nazism but to two factors: the jealous vigilance of a chief of army general staff determined to keep control of military planning and not take orders from the Wehrmachtamt of the War Ministry, an attitude which Müller believes explains why he disobeyed orders in 1935 and 1937 to draw up plans for an attack on Czechoslovakia; and, secondly, Beck's conviction that Hitler's tactics in the summer of 1938 were ill considered and likely to end in a disastrous war certain to set Germany back in her plans for dominating Europe. Resentful though he was that the general staff had not been consulted by Hitler as it had been by William II in 1914, Beck did not plan to overthrow Hitler, as Hoffmann and others before him have alleged; on the contrary, completely misunderstanding the type of man he was facing, Beck talked of a 'strike of the generals', but simply to save the Führer from his evil advisers. Only after his resignation did it dawn on him that Hitler himself was the root cause of the trouble, and only then did Beck move to a resistance posture properly so called.

Müller's reinterpretation, which he has successfully defended against heavy attack, does not diminish Beck's stature, as the author demonstrates in the final essay on the military opposition to Hitler.[7] Hoffmann is surely wide of the mark when he censures

Müller on the grounds that 'the negative evaluation of the plots against Hitler and of the participants in them is a particular instance of a comprehensive attempt to explain historical events on the basis of class affiliations. . . . The impulses which arise out of patriotism and a national outlook . . . end up as matters of secondary importance if they are evaluated in "class" terms which sell historical reality short.'[8] Müller does not deny that a sense of moral outrage can move men to action. What he is saying is that a historian cannot be content with explanations of complex historical phenomena which rely heavily on subjective moral judgements of individual actions and which cannot account adequately for divergent human responses to a common problem. Nor does Peter Hüttenberger's formula defining resistance as action by a part of a ruling group against the dominant part[9] resolve the matter satisfactorily, though it is perhaps a step in the right direction. Only within a properly structured multi-dimensional framework which defines the political and social aims and objectives of the *dramatis personae*, as Müller tries to do, can one begin to understand the interaction between moral imperatives activating the individual and secular politics of which he is a part; only then can one see Beck – or any other historical figure, for that matter – not through a distorting mirror as saint or villain but 'warts and all'. That is what history is all about.

Notes

1 *Nazi Conspiracy and Aggression: Opinion and Judgment* (Washington, D.C., 1947), p. 107. For the opinion of the dissenting Russian judge L. T. Nikitchenko cf. pp. 183–8.
2 Cf. Telford Taylor, *Sword and Swastika: Generals and Nazis in the Third Reich* (New York, 1952).
3 R. O'Neill, *The German Army and the Nazi Party, 1933–39* (London, 1966), p. 172.
4 C. Streit, *op. cit.*, p. 300.
5 Cf. H. Boog, J. Förster, J. Hoffmann, E. Klink, R-D Müller and Gerd R. Ueberschär, *Das Deutsche Reich und der Zweite Weltkrieg. 4. Der Angriff auf die Sowjetunion* (Freiburg, 1983), chapters V and VII.
6 Cf. W. Deist, *The Wehrmacht and German Rearmament*, with a foreword by A. J. Nicholls (London, 1981).
7 By Peter Hoffman, in *Historische Zeitschrift* 234 (1982), pp. 101–21. Cf. K-J Müller's reply in 235, pp. 355–71.
8 Peter Hoffman, *Historische Zeitschrift* 234 (1982), p. 101.
9 See Hüttenberger, note 6 at p. 117 below.

Chronology

1933

January Adolf Hitler appointed German chancellor.
October Germany leaves Disarmament Conference and League of Nations. Beck appointed head of Truppenamt (a front for what was actually the general staff).

1934

February Fritsch appointed commander-in-chief of the army.
June Murder of SA leaders in the 'night of the long knives'.
August Death of Hindenburg: Hitler assumes title of Leader and Chancellor; army swears oath of personal allegiance to Hitler.

1935

March Hitler announces reintroduction of one-year conscription; Germany to have peacetime army of thirty-six divisions.
July Beck's Truppenamt officially named General Staff of the Army.

1936

March Reoccupation of demilitarised Rhineland.
August Period of conscription increased to two years.

1937

November Hitler reveals to top advisers at Hossbach conference his intention to seize Austria and Czechoslovakia in near future.

December	Priority in military strategy given to pre-emptive strike at Czechoslovakia (Plan Green).

1938

February	Blomberg–Fritsch crisis; Blomberg, Minister of War, and Fritsch, commander-in-chief of army, removed from their posts; Hitler becomes commander-in-chief of Wehrmacht; Brauchitsch appointed commander-in-chief of army.
March	Annexation of Austria
August	Resignation of Beck and appointment of Halder as chief of army general staff.
September	Munich conference ends crisis over Czechoslovakia.

1939

March	Hitler seizes 'Rump' Czechoslovakia.
September	Attack on Poland and beginning of second world war.

1940

April	Seizure of Norway and Denmark
May	Attack on France, Belgium and Holland.
June	Capitulation of France.

1941

June	Attack on Russia
December	Hitler takes over from Brauchitsch as commander-in-chief of army.

1942

September	Halder replaced as chief of army general staff by Zeitzler.

1943

January	Surrender of Sixth Army at Stalingrad.

1944

June	Anglo-American landing in Normandy.
July	Bomb plot; execution of Beck and others in aftermath. Zeitzler replaced as chief of army general staff by Guderian.

1945

April   Suicide of Hitler.
May   Surrender of German armed forces to allied powers.

The army and the Third Reich
An essay in historical interpretation

I

From the very moment when the formation of Hitler's government inaugurated the Third Reich the relationship between the army and National Socialism preoccupied contemporaries. The question of the army's role in Hitler's state, more particularly the question of the influence it had, or could have had, over the development of the Nazi regime, has preoccupied political observers and historians ever since.[1]

Scarcely a year after the so-called 'seizure of power' the French ambassador in Berlin, André François-Poncet, reflected: 'Two institutions, the German army and the National Socialist party, found themselves face to face, . . . the question was, who would gain the upper hand in the new German state, the party or the army.'[2] The French diplomat's words forcibly underline the political weight and historical significance which contemporary observers were inclined to ascribe to the army for the future of the Nazi state. A few years later, in early January 1937, a memorandum from conservative circles critical of the regime was played into the hands of the army high command which stated: 'Responsibility for the future course of events rests with the army alone. There is no avoiding this conclusion. Opinion at home and abroad is at one in this, and with justice.'[3]

So it is only too understandable that after the defeat of the Reich and the collapse of the regime the problem of the army's relationship to it should have been posed with new insistence, entangled with the question of the responsibility of the military. The army was on trial in a double sense. The High Command and the General Staff, both as institutions and — in the case of leading military personnel — as individuals, found themselves reunited in the dock at Nuremberg. Almost simultaneously there began the 'trial of history': the debate among historians, on the basis of a rapidly growing body of source material, about the role of the army in Germany's most recent past.

The framework within which political discussion and historical reflection alike took place was that of liberal constitutionalism. The principal charge — that the army had interfered inadmissibly in politics and society, had in fact come to dominate them and thus shared the blame for Hitler's regime and its deeds – is itself evidence of this form of constitutionalism. Such constitutionalism is based on the idea of the military executive as instrumental in character and under the strict civil control of the political leadership, and on the idea of a separation between the sphere of the military and that of those entrusted with political sovereignty in civilian society.

The same frame of reference, and judgement, is reflected, albeit indirectly, in the generally apologetic interventions of former officers,[4] for example when it was argued, as it often was, that the army had been misused by a criminally irresponsible political leadership and dragged to disaster against its own better instincts.

Drawing on a different theory of democracy but issuing in an analogous form of argument is the thesis that the failure of the military leadership in the face of the challenge from Hitler can be blamed on the narrowly professional outlook which developed in the Wilhelmine Reich and reached its zenith in the Seeckt era of the Weimar Republic.

Many books published in the 1940s and 1950s reflect similar conceptions in their titles: *Guilt and Catastrophe*, *Nemesis of Power*, *Army in Chains* and *Command in Conflict*. Phrases like these demonstrate how the theme, treated against the background of such a view of the constitution and of democracy, usually came to be seen in moral and political terms. In addition a highly personal perspective was often evident. Another book is entitled – characteristically – *Field Marshal Keitel: Criminal or Officer?*[5]

For all that, moral and political categories simply do not possess adequate rational power of explanation for historical analysis of issues of such complexity. It is necessary to derive a categorical frame of reference which will permit a sufficiently rational analysis and explanation of the events and their interconnections, and make historical assimilation possible. This is not to suggest that the political and moral issues posed by the relationship of the army to the Nazi state are to be repressed or denied. Only our historical knowledge, by elucidating fundamental facts and providing appropriate classificatory criteria, can furnish a sound enough basis for the formulation and mastery of the political and moral issues involved.

From a historical perspective two elements helpful in forming the necessary frame of reference stand out: on the one hand, the feudal Junker tradition of the Prusso-German military state;[6] on the other, industrial society organised on capitalist lines. The circumstances of each phase of the army's confrontation with National Socialism during the late '20s and early '30s were decisively determined by these two elements. They did not function independently of one another but stood in a complex, multi-levelled, reciprocal relationship.[7] In very general terms the German state of the late nineteenth and early twentieth centuries can be defined as a dynamic industrial society, founded and led by the predominantly agrarian, pre-industrial feudal Junker elite. Those who by education and economic position constituted the middle class had largely adopted the social attitudes of this elite and identified with its socio-economic interests.[8] In this 'unfinished nation state'[9] other strata of society remained excluded from decisions fundamental to political and social life, or were only inadequately made party to them. This was true not only of the ethnic minorities, such as the Danes, the Poles and the people of Alsace-Lorraine, but also of those who gathered under the banner of social democracy, as well as for large sections of the Catholic population – at least for a while.

Here one of the principal problems of the new Reich becomes discernible. The fact that Germany's industrial revolution coincided with the founding of the state under the leadership of a still feudal Prussia left the new nation with a problem fundamental to its existence: that of integration. The new Reich not only had to unify a number of recently independent states (*Länder*), each shaped by its own individual history. It had at the same time to reconcile an old ruling elite, the new social classes, and elements of traditional society which had been transformed by the process of industrialisation. This difficulty was accentuated by the pace of industrial development. Moreover the gulf between the 'feudal' and 'feudalised' elites on one hand and those who had no voice in government on the other was not the only barrier that had to be overcome. There were conflicts of interest within the ruling class as

well as between it and the rest of society. Headlong industrialisation increased the intensity and complexity of these differences.
The problem of integration thus became an essential, if not the
decisive, structural feature of the Prusso-German nation state. The
many and varied attempts to engineer secondary integration and
political stability — government repression, thoughts of *coups
d'état*, ideological and organisational mobilisation of the masses —
never entirely resolved the problem, bearing witness instead to the
persistent fragility of the political and social structure.[10]

The problem of integration thus forms a central element in the
historical frame of reference within which the problem of the army
and National Socialism is to be situated. Under the constitution the
Prusso-German army was an army of universal conscription. Yet it
was led by an officer corps which regarded itself not only as a
professional but also as a social and political elite.[11] The officer
corps was an integral part of the traditional social and political
leadership caste of the Prusso-German state. It constituted a recognised group within the traditional, pre-industrial ruling elite and
shared its legitimating values. This is reflected in the exceptional,
semi-autonomous status of the military command *vis-à-vis* the
government as the political and administrative executive. This
independence, this dualism of the military and the political and
administrative leadership, overcome only in the person of the
monarch, was inherited from the old Prussian military monarchy
and is a characteristic feature of the Prusso-German state. Its historical importance can scarcely be overestimated.[12] It was the officers'
special position within the state, their standing as political elite, that
determined not only their self-conception but their attitude to the
state and to society even after the monarchy's collapse. Because of its
distinct image of itself and its prominent position within the state,
the officer corps was particularly exposed to the tensions inherent in
the structure of the new nation state. In other words, the problem of
integration affected not only the professional but also the social and
political legitimacy of the officer corps.

A second major element in the historical frame of reference can
be derived from a sequence of developments associated with the
'technological industrialism' already mentioned. Technological
development based on advances in science and their application to
industry in a rapidly growing economy had revolutionary consequences for the nature of the military and of warfare that went far

beyond the changed relation of time and space, increased capacity for destruction of the new weapons that were being developed.

The 'mechanisation' and 'industrialisation' of the military and of war is thus our second main point of reference.[13] In essence, technical developments brought about a fundamental shift in the balance that had always existed between ends and means in the deployment of armed force. Once technological development had reached a certain level the destructive power of weaponry meant that it could no longer be used in a controlled manner, step by step, to achieve finite, limited objectives.

At the same time the need to ensure technological excellence, to promote mass production and the mobilisation of all national resources, led the military to make growing demands on more and more sectors of the economy and society. The result was a tendency for the military and the civilian spheres to converge: the military and the conduct of war become once more an influence that affected the whole of society. In the final analysis this meant that the *ratio essendi* of military power, as an instrument for the realisation of political aims, was destroyed.[14]

This problem, in principle one that affected all the industrialised great powers, confronted the Prusso-German state and its army in particularly acute form. The Prussian-German position in the international system was especially precarious in so far as the basic line Bismarck had chosen — namely to pursue a great-power policy without firm alliance to any one partner — still required consolidation through military force. Thus the external dimensions of the question of consolidation (defending the country and pursuing acts of war) became interlaced with that of consolidation within (integration and legitimation). The challenge of technical/industrial development processes had a substantial effect on both these complex problems.

In concrete terms this meant that the officer corps faced a double challenge. On the one hand it was responsible, as a professional and a socio-political elite, for the optimal preparation, organisation and conduct of a kind of warfare which, under the conditions of an industrialised economy, had taken on a new dimension. On the other, precisely this industrial and technological change in the nature of the army and of warfare posed a threat to its professionalism in so far as only society as a whole could ensure the complete effectiveness of the military machine in a future total war.

The experts' claim to professional exclusivity could no longer be sustained in the face of a 'total' war. A species of division of labour was the inescapable prospect for those who regarded themselves as officers and gentlemen. Given their position in the Prusso-German military state, this undermining of the professionalism of the military meant also the questioning of its position as a socio-political elite, and thus a threat to one of the constituent elements in the whole power structure.

Such a crucial challenge was made even more serious by the mechanisation of the armed forces and the consequent breakdown of the cohesion hitherto characteristic of the military as a national leadership class. As the war machine became more complex and differentiated the military elite was itself forced to become more specialised and differentiated. What it amounted to was widespread specialisation in the armed services. The general staff took on the increasingly important role of general management, a technocratic planning and directorial function closely akin to that of large industrial organisations. Technical specialists, as in effect the engineer and warrant officers of the navy were, answered the demands of new technical developments. The line officers themselves, whose authority had derived largely from the unquestioned supremacy of the old order, could not escape the performance and efficiency standards set by the growing complexity of the military apparatus, with its numerous new branches – aviation, telecommunications, modern artillery, railway operation, machine-gun corps, mine-laying, etc. Thus was reflected the divergence between the general staff and line officers, between the old branches of the service like the cavalry and the new ones, or, in the navy, with its sophisticated technology, the division into general service, technical and warrant officers – a necessary concomitant of the process of modernisation. The drawback, the other side of the coin, was that these developments meant the disintegration of a patrician military caste which had once been distinguished simply by its 'aristocratic professional standing', its leadership qualities, finding in that status its inward unity and cohesion.

In retrospect a glance at the first world war, which ended for Germany in defeat and revolution, makes clear the determining influence of the two points of reference which we have stressed on historical development. The unsolved problem of integration revealed its gravity in the collapse of the power structure under the shock of war. Hereditary authority was not alone in its fate. The

revolution struck directly at the military – for it too was representative of the establishment.

The first world war, as the first 'mechanised industrial' conflict
involving the whole of society, undermined the professionalism of
the military elite in quite concrete ways. The social expansion of the
recruitment reservoir of the officer corps to include war reserve
officers, together with the creation of service ranks which performed
officer duties without actually possessing the rank (cf. the hybrid
ranks of 'deputy' officers and sergeant-major lieutenants), are symptomatic of the process, as are the assumption by professional soldiers
of what were strictly speaking civilian roles such as civil administration, economic planning and organisation, and the exercise of the
command by non-professionals (reserve officers).

The war thus accentuated both the problem of integration and
the problems of technological industrialisation of the military and
of warfare. War and revolution resulted in a profound questioning
of the system of political rule as well as the social system in which
the Prusso-German officer corps came into being and evolved. At
the same time the inner unity of the officer corps was disintegrating
as warfare became mechanised and industrialised. It is this coincidence, this twofold challenge which was the decisive factor in the
future development of the officer corps.[15]

The revolution and the reorganisation of the state after 1918 did
nothing to remove these problems. The old military elite, like other
sections of the traditional power structure, was able to maintain its
hereditary position despite the process of relativisation introduced
by the parliamentary republic; the structural problems they faced,
although they appeared in different guise, were not fundamentally
altered. The problem of integration in certain respects became more
acute and the secular challenge posed by social, technological and
economic change was in no way diminished.

It is within such a historical frame of reference that the subsequent complex developments at various levels in the confrontation
of the traditional military elite and National Socialism must be seen
and understood.

II

It is conceivable that after the defeat of the Wilhelmine Reich the
military elite could have transferred its concerns to the purely

professional task of ensuring that the armed services were fully
equipped to meet the demands of modern, 'total war'.[16] Instead –
and this is our first thesis – it responded to the secular challenge of
war, defeat and the downfall of the monarchy by determinedly
attempting to hold on to the basic elements of its historical past.
With hindsight it appears that the military elite failed to take the
potential way out which it might have, in changing from an elite
both professional and political to a purely professional one of
military specialists. Even this move would not have overcome the
fundamental challenge to its existence posed by the advent of a type
of warfare which involved the whole of society. If the collapse of
the monarchy did not change the priorities of the military elite, it
did alter the problem of its legitimation. The problem of
legitimising its claims to remain a social and political elite loomed
even larger as a result of new political circumstances and the
experience of the first mechanised, industrialised war.

With the political and military collapse of 1918 this was at first
concealed by the conflict within the officer corps over its position
relative to the revolution and to the reconstruction of the state and
of political life. Those in the officer corps who favoured restoration
of the monarchy were defeated in 1920 in the Kapp-Lüttwitz
putsch. Those who supported nationalist revolution, drawn mostly
from the Freikorps, failed to emerge as a serious force because of
their own fragmentation and the relatively swift consolidation of
the republic. Many were later to be found in the SA and the SS.[17]
A third tendency, the 'wait and see' attitude of Seeckt, prevailed.

At the root of this dispute lay the essential problem of legitimation, to which each of the three groups had an answer. Those who
wanted to see the monarchy restored wished to re-establish the
political and social *status quo ante*. The nationalist revolutionaries
sought to combine military professionalism *and* political leadership
in an image of the 'political soldier' – or, more correctly, the
'political warrior' (*Krieger*) – and sought to attain new, if
somewhat vaguely conceived, social and political structures.
Seeckt's 'wait and see' posture, on the other hand, was an attempt
to maintain under changed political and military circumstances the
traditional claim of the officer corps to be not only a professional
but a social and political elite. The allegiance of the army (Reichswehr) officer corps to an abstract ideal of the state far removed
from the realities of the Republic, as encouraged by Seeckt, was a

means of registering its claim to autonomy *vis-à-vis* parliamentary government as well as an expression of the claim to semi-independent political elite status. This traditional claim to constitute an elite manifested itself in Seeckt's view that in the armed deployment of the military in the interests of the Republic between 1919 and 1923 the military retained its claim to autonomy. It was this same claim to autonomy which was behind Seeckt's refusal in the Kapp-Lüttwitz *putsch* to place the army's existence at risk for the benefit of the constitutional government.

Thus in no sense can it be said that the military elite directed its attention solely to the optimal preparation for and conduct of modern mechanised, industrial warfare, a form of warfare which in undermining military professionalism was itself a profound challenge even to the purely military specialist. On the contrary, the Prusso-German military elite by-passed the challenge to its professionalism by virtue of its traditional claim to political leadership and a share in the responsibility for government. By clinging to its political claims the military attempted to master the political upheavals of 1918–19 as well as to solve the problem of the erosion of military professionalism by modern warfare. Its historical role as a political elite, embodied in the Prusso-German dualism of political and military leadership, continued after 1918 under changed conditions. It was precisely modern warfare, involving all of society, that provided a new legitimation for the traditional claim of the political military elite to a share in the responsible leadership of the state. If the officer corps constituted an essentially political elite it could play an authoritative and responsible role in the political leadership of the nation in preparing for mechanised, industrial total war. If it saw itself as a purely professional elite it would have been devoured by a type of warfare which was no longer the province of the military profession alone but would engulf the whole of society. Because the military considered itself an elite with political responsibility, part of the social and political leadership, the nature of modern warfare, which in its totality allowed of no 'warrior' vocation for the military profession, could not affect its existence in principle. The political tradition of the Prusso-German military elite thus saved the military from any fundamental undermining by the phenomenon of modern warfare. The history of the officer corps and the developments in the relationship of the military, the state and society were thus not determined exclusively by the rise of modern warfare, but also to a large extent by the continuation of the political traditions of the Prusso-German officer corps.[18] Precisely as a result of this political tradition the removal of the division between the civilian and the military spheres of responsibility as a result of total warfare became a strong motive for maintaining traditional claims to leadership.

Several symptoms bear out these findings. One of the causes of the increased functional and social narrowness of the officer corps was undoubtedly the attempt to restore the homogeneity which had been broken by the war and which was an important precondition of the claim to a political elite status. The post-war army, the Reichswehr, was more strongly dominated by a leadership drawn from the nobility and the bourgeoisie than had been the case before or during the war. The instinct for self-preservation among this elite is striking. Whereas the percentage of officers' sons among officer recruits had fallen in the period from 1880 to 1913 from 30 to 28 per cent, it rose from 44 to 55 per cent between 1926 and 1930.[19] Although the mechanised battles of the first world war had given rise to a new type of officer – delineated in literary form by Ernst Junger and Walter Flex, among others – the Reichswehr was overwhelmingly commanded by men who came originally from the Prussian Guards, many indeed from one particular Guards regiment, the famous 3rd Foot, and who belonged, almost without exception, to the general staff.[20] Neither the pure 'warrior' type nor the 'political soldier' featured among the leadership of the Reichswehr. Instead the general staff, both in person and as an ideal, became the vehicle which carried over into the Republic the claim to status as a political elite and as a functional and professional body which could responsibly plan and direct the complete mobilisation of society necessary for modern warfare.

Nor did war, defeat, revolution or the post-war era evoke any essential modifications in the basic political goals and ideals of the military elite. In fact those goals emerged more clearly cut and unequivocal. There were indeed considerable differences over tactics and methods, but in its essential elements the continuity of aims remained unbroken.

In the realm of foreign policy a position as a great power, or, more precisely, the recovery of the Reich's position as a great power in a Europe transformed by Versailles, was certainly sought.[21] Although differences existed within the military elite over how this might be realised in detail, there was agreement about general objectives. There was agreement, too, that every opportunity of furthering them should be exploited to the utmost. Although there were differences in unscrupulousness or sense of responsibility, and in willingness to take risks, among such diverse representatives of the military elite as Groener, Blomberg and Beck, when they contemplated changing the power structures of Europe, on one point at least they were united. Groener's directive of April 1930 on the 'tasks of the Armed Forces' and Blomberg's in summer 1937 'on the concerted preparation of the armed forces for war'[22] both alike embodied the idea that in favourable international circumstances, and regardless of the army's relative weakness, the use of military means for the realisation of Germany's claim to be a great power should be foreseen or at least considered. 'An unprovoked offensive deployment of the Reichswehr was not excluded, where the risks remained calculable.'[23] That was also General Beck's view in 1937/38, with some reservations.[24] The line of continuity in the idea of Germany as a great power supported by the military is evident.

In the realm of domestic policy the basic model on which the political aims of the military were based was that of an authoritarian state, however it was conceived in detail. Apart from the influence of traditional ideas, two motivating factors played a role: one was to stabilise the leadership position of the traditional elites rather better than could be expected under a parliamentary system, the other was to be capable of meeting as fully as possible the demands of 'total war', the new mechanised, industrial warfare. Even here there is a striking continuity of aims, despite differences in detail and in prevailing circumstances. A direct line connects Seeckt's ideas[25] on the army's role in the state and his plans for state reform with Groener's dictum that in German political life 'not a single stone should be turned without the word of the Reichswehr having tipped the scales'.[26] There was a close connection between the objectives of foreign and domestic policy. In an important memorandum of 29 December 1923 Seeckt suggested to the Minister of the Interior that the state of emergency which had been proclaimed and the Reich's planned intervention in matters normally reserved to the Länder should be exploited to reorganise the Reich's internal structure along centralised, authoritarian lines. He continued, with a clear reference to the implications for foreign policy: 'when all is said and done, we are dealing with the great German problem: if we wish to pursue the politics of a great power we must eliminate waste in all areas – it is particularly gross because of the Reich's federal structure (about ninety Ministers and over 2,100 elected representatives) . . .'.[27] Almost six years later Schleicher remarked that the armed forces had 'to preserve their pre-eminent, determining role in future developments in the areas of foreign and domestic policy'.[28]

Whoever led the Reichswehr, all these generals and Ministers – the Social Democrat Noske being the only exception – pursued two essentially unwavering political aims, only priorities and methods differing according to the situation and the individual. The first was to share political power by participating in fundamental political decision-making. The other was to enable Germany to pursue her policies as a great power supported by military strength.

Admittedly it became apparent towards the end of the Weimar Republic that these political claims and objectives had led the Reichswehr to a dead end. It became evident then that the problem of integration, far from being solved, had, under the strain of the consequences of war and the economic crisis, become dangerously acute, not least because the socio-economic structures themselves had not escaped their internal tensions under the changed national political situation.

With its claim to political elite status and to a voice in the determination and realisation of political goals, the leadership of the Reichswehr risked being drawn into the increasing polarisation of internal arguments. In view of the relationship of power, responsible army leaders recognised the impossibility of pursuing their political ambitions to the point of a trial of strength with large sectors of society, perhaps even against certain groups whose interests and prestige, under certain circumstances, matched their own.[29] Moreover there were signs that it was becoming increasingly difficult to preserve the unity of the officer corps on the basis of Seeckt's ideas. Although Seeckt's firm hand had once managed to bring about the necessary unity, the use of internal repression was found to have its limits to the extent to which the 'state within a state' ideology lost its unifying power. The effort at political subversion by young officers of an Ulm artillery regiment, which earned them an indictment for high treason and conviction in the Supreme Court at Leipzig, was alarmingly symptomatic. The lieutenants' conspiracy revealed not only a youthful activism and the widely aired antagonism between the 'desk-bound generals' in Berlin and officers of the line, but also the outlines of an alternative conception, albeit a confused and romantic one, of the role of the officer as a 'political soldier', bound to the people and committed to the 'national revolution'. Any such concept would not only have hastened the disintegration but would also have drawn the army into internal political confrontations.[30]

The leaders of the Reichswehr came increasingly to recognise the gulf that was opening up between their political aspirations and their ability to realise them. At this point the unresolved problem of integration resurfaced with new acuteness. Not only had the traditional elites' basis of popular support been eroded, they no longer had at their disposal the various means of stabilising the situation which before the war had sustained the illusion that they were still in some way masters of the situation. Developments in domestic politics in the late 1920s made their inability to do so more apparent.

General von Schleicher was still attempting on the one hand to create a new political base by bringing together the so-called left wing of the National Socialists under Strasser and the trade unions, and on the other to give the army a social base by, among other things, the project of a state youth training programme organised primarily by the military. This was meant to spare the Reichswehr an open struggle for power within the state which it saw itself in no position to win. But Schleicher failed.[31]

This dead-end situation in domestic as well as national politics was further exacerbated by the fact that the army had reached a decisive juncture in both military policy and military expertise which called for fundamental decisions affecting both internal and external policy.[32] Already by 1928 a first rearmament programme which set out priorities and systematically integrated all available resources had been set in motion. In the summer of 1930 preparations began for a second programme, which was approved by the military and their political masters early in 1932. The crucial problem in planning rearmament and military policy was recruitment. From 1931 on trained classes would no longer be available in sufficient numbers for the planned field army of twenty-one divisions. The stopgaps contemplated touched on the vital questions of a revision of the Versailles treaty and of defence strategy (e.g. the Reichswehr as a professional army under the Treaty of Versailles should be supplemented by some form of militia raised by limited conscription). Thus the fundamental question of Germany's future foreign policy in the role of a great power was adumbrated alongside the central issue of the relation to political power of the military elite.

Hence the question of political and social integration was linked once again with that of international power politics, its methods and possibilities in an age of technical and industrial warfare, in a complex of problems which not only determined the political circumstances under which Hitler's government was formed but which also revealed the long-term historical perspective in which the events of 30 January 1933 must be seen.

III

Such a historical perspective allows us to formulate a second thesis: Hitler's government was formed in 1933 on the basis of an *entente* between elements of the traditional elite and the leadership of the Hitler movement. Within this *entente* the Reichswehr had a unique position and carried special weight.

Each of the parties to it saw particular advantages for themselves and their specific interests. The old elites were no longer capable of maintaining their traditional position alone or of realising their political objectives inside or outside Germany. They lacked the necessary social base. And Hitler – or so it seemed to the advocates of an alliance with the National Socialists – could bring them that essential mass base, thereby solving the problem of integration for them. For his part, Hitler was forced to the realisation that he could never achieve power on the strength of his own support. 9 November 1923 had proved the impossibility of a *coup d'état*. The elections of November 1932 demonstrated the impossibility of obtaining power through a parliamentary majority. The mass movement had brought him to the threshold of power: but only the old power elites, which still held a decisive position in the power apparatus, could help him cross this threshold. Only they could help him to a share in power.

In this situation the army not only assumed a key role, it also maintained a prominent and an *apparently* strong position within the *entente*. It could rely on Field Marshal President von Hinden-

burg, whose prerogatives – among them those of the supreme
commander of the armed forces – lay beyond the reach of the Nazi
movement. Hindenburg made General von Blomberg, an army man
and an officer he trusted, Minister of Defence. Hitler had no
opportunity of choosing independently the Minister of Defence in
his Cabinet. More than that, he was obliged to promise to refrain
from any interference in army matters.[33] This was not simply an act
of political prudence on the part of Hitler's coalition partners. Nor
was it simply an expression of Hindenburg's desire to safeguard his
constitutional prerogatives. The move was in line with the Prusso-
German dualism of the military and the political: both components
of the state again stood side by side, united in the last instance in the
person of the 'substitute monarch', Hindenburg. In this respect the
structure of the old Prusso-German empire was thus apparently
re-established under a different set of circumstances. In this regard
the appointment of General von Blomberg and his political adviser,
Colonel von Reichenau, to head the Ministry of Defence did not
represent a fundamental change but only – alongside a change of
personnel – a tactical political alternative to someone like Schleicher or Seeckt. Hitler took pains to emphasise, by manipulation
and propaganda, the supposed resumption of the Prusso-German
structural principle by adopting the formula that the new Reich
rested on 'twin pillars', the army and the party. This 'twin-pillar'
concept had a considerable psychological impact, both within the
army and outside it, which should not be underestimated.[34]

Thus, the army appeared at the time to be not merely a strong
bulwark, not merely a political counterweight to the mass populism
of the Hitler movement. It appeared to be once more an autonomous political factor. Precisely for this reason the overwhelming
majority of the officer corps – or so it appears – were in agreement
with the so-called 'National Coalition', despite minor reservations.
The new regime appeared to promise what the old elites no longer
felt capable of achieving alone: the nationalist integration of the
overwhelming majority of the nation and the suppression of the
rest. In the first place, the Reichswehr thus escaped the struggle for
power within Germany which was feared: it could once again
regard its position, which had become increasingly precarious, as
secure. Secondly, the integration of the nation under Hitler's
government seemed to grant the preconditions for a comprehensive
solution to the problems posed by mechanised industrial warfare.

Thirdly, there was a desire to believe that the leadership role of the army had been secured by the supposed re-establishment of its quasi-autonomous political power. The domestic political conditions for the realisation of the foreign policy objectives of a great power appeared to have been met.

It was for these reasons that the leaders of the new Reichswehr supported Hitler in the consolidation of the new regime.[35] They looked on 'neutrally', i.e. supportively, as he first suppressed the left, then eliminated the bourgeois parties, centralised the political and administrative structure of the Reich and so appeared to realise the political ideal of an authoritarian, centralised state. The politically privileged position of the army seemed assured, but it was relieved of the task, which was in any case beyond it, of giving that position a social and political foundation.

IV

In the light of these developments a third thesis can be put forward: contrary to the view still held, we can assert that there were at the time no differences of opinion within the military leadership about the basic form the coalition with Hitler should take.[36] Differences might arise over the tactics and methods by which the model might actually be developed. From 1934 on there was confrontations, at times violent, between the army command (Heeresführung) under Generals von Fritsch and Beck on the one hand and the armed forces command (Wehrmachtführung) under Blomberg and Reichenau on the other. The army command tended to define the coalition with the National Socialists in a rather restrictive way. It believed it could best serve the army's interests and those of the traditional military elite by trying to preserve as many as possible of the traditional values of old, conservative Prusso-Germany in the new political situation. In this specific sense the commander-in-chief, General von Fritsch, considered himself a 'mediator between old and new'. One of his closest collaborators, the Armed Forces' Chief Adjutant to Hitler and head of the Central Department of General Staff, Colonel, then General Hossbach, described Fritsch's policy thus: the army leadership was guided by the idea of 'building on the sure foundations of the past and adapting to the changed spirit of the times'.[37] Fritsch issued a string of orders and directives in which he combined an affirmation of loyalty to the new regime

with a stress on the tested values of Prussian tradition. He believed
that only by safeguarding those traditional values could the position of the military elite in the new state be guaranteed. In no sense
did he dispute the Nazi character of the state, but he understood it
as a state based on an alliance of old and new, in which it was
incumbent on the army to represent the standpoint and values of
the traditional elite.

Fritsch's politics were the restrictive, emphatically conservative
version of the co-operation of the military elite and National
Socialism.

The men of the armed forces command (Wehrmachtführung)
were quite different. They were in favour of co-operation and
collaboration without much regard to traditional values and practices if that was the only way in which the military elite could be
assured of a decisive influence in the new regime. Reichenau coined
the slogan: 'Into the new state, so as to maintain the position which
is our due'.[38] The reference to the 'position which is our due'
expresses openly the claim of the traditional military elite to a share
in political power. But Reichenau also observed, '. . . Not even the
most boneheaded reactionary could expect us to turn back the
wheel of history today. . . . [The whole state] is in sure hands. . . .
And we, with our seven obsolete divisions scattered across the
country, are supposed to pull something out of the bag? Only an
idiot could think it! We are accustomed to face facts sensibly! . . .
There remained practically only one way open to us: to face facts as
they were.'

This view of the position set him apart from Fritsch. Reichenau
saw the new balance of power and socio-political change as so
profound and irreversible that they went beyond the claims of old
values and the tested 'sure foundations of the past'. For this reason
he had no scruples about sacrificing the holiest cows of Prussian
tradition when it was necessary to preserve or strengthen the army's
political power. The Minister, von Blomberg, was of the same
mind. For, if he acted less out of machiavellian calculation than
from fascination with the 'national dynamism' Hitler had kindled,
he too was prepared to integrate the army into the 'new state'.

It was thus that the Nazi symbols such as the sovereign eagle
appeared alongside the swastika in the armed forces, and it was
thus that inhuman ideological concessions of a legally dubious
nature were made, such as the introduction of the 'Aryan par-

agraph' in consequence of which nearly a hundred 'non-Aryan' officers and men were got rid of.[39] It was thus that there was no reaction in the armed forces command when Hitler violated or abolished basic human and civil rights. Instead Reichenau in ice-cold calculation explained to the officer corps that the army stood to gain more from the abolition of freedom of the press than it would lose.[40] By means of carefully directed propaganda and progressively introduced indoctrination and ideology, initiated and controlled not by the party but by the military command, the Minister and his political adviser strove to make the army not merely an integral part of the new regime but equal partner of the party, with scant regard to traditional values.

The difference of emphasis between the chief-in-command of the army and the responsible leaders of the armed forces can be perceived in the decrees on the image of the officer and on the educational principles of the officer corps. In one such order, for example, Blomberg demanded 'comradeship and community of spirit' with representatives of Nazi organisations, denouncing the 'isolationism of military leaders' and their position as 'masters clinging to out-of-date ideas'. Fritsch, on the other hand, referred all commanders to the exemplary order of the commander of the 1st Panzer Division, General Baron von Weichs, which stated that with the seizure of power by the Nazis 'our whole nation [*Volk*], not only outwardly but in its spiritual attitudes, has begun to march in step with the army'. An officer was therefore 'a symbol and a representative of the German way of life'. In these words the general gave the claim to constitute an elite influential beyond the professional, military sphere its classic formulation. In the same vein, he continued, pride in one's position might indeed be arrogant, but only the 'officer conscious of his class' could be a 'spiritually free personality' belonging to a 'group specially chosen, specially tested and with special obligations'.[41]

Despite such differences of emphasis, army command and armed forces command reacted equally firmly whenever members of the party threatened to encroach on their sphere. In their view, this would have contravened the assumption, fundamental to the military elite's claim to autonomy, that they were partners with equal rights. Thus Reichenau, speaking to officers of the army corps in winter 1935, voiced his opinion of the growing volume of reproaches from the party and the SS in terms as forceful as they were characteristic. 'We do not need to make the soldier into a National Socialist . . . We are National Socialists without party cards . . . the best and most serious.' Revolutionary spirit, which some 'reformers from the Hitler Youth and SA' had tried to introduce into the army, had no place there. The armed forces were 'the single, last and greatest hope of the Führer'. Conversely National Socialists entering the army still had first to be made into soldiers.

The army command and the leadership of the armed forces thus agreed in principle on affirming the new regime and on the position due to the army. They had different views, however, on tactics and methods.

The differences over method reflected, moreover, different attitudes to the modern world. General von Fritsch represented more a stance rooted in pre-industrial feudalism. He set much store by old values and ideals, and accepted reluctantly what he is said to have called 'all those damnable innovations, cars, tanks, etc.'. The breeding and character of the officer cadets were more important to him than their school-leaving certificates (*Abitur*), that bourgeois proof of qualification.[42] The armed forces command, on the other hand, was of opinion that the world had changed, and that the old elite would have to modify its values if it wanted to survive. Fritsch's attitude was more static and defensive. Blomberg and especially Reichenau thought more dynamically but also more unscrupulously. Fritsch and his followers were representative of a continuity of old feudal values in a changed environment, whereas his opponents in the military embodied rather the continuity in military power politics.

The two groups represent two different answers to the difficult question of how the traditional elites might preserve their former position in a rapidly changing world. They were at one in *making* the claim to traditional leadership, even in politics. Without doubt the differences over tactics and methods between the army command and the leadership of the army were one reason for Hitler's total success in gradually eliminating the army as a politically relevant factor, in eventually suppressing it completely and finally making it a simple, though thoroughly effective, instrument of his policies. Their different views on methods and tactics impaired the unequivocal unity of leadership and destroyed the ideological coherence of the military leadership cadres in a rapidly changing social and political environment.

The main reason for Hitler's success in depriving the army of political power lay in the fundamental political changes brought about by the Führer and his party, and in the real or imagined social change they created. The military elite's position was weakened disastrously by Hitler's accumulation of powerful political functions such as his assumption, upon Hindenberg's death, of the presidency of the Reich, a role crucial to the army. The armed forces now swore an oath of allegiance to the person of the 'Führer and the Reich Chancellor'. The introduction of universal conscription swiftly expanded the army and further undermined the homogeneity of the old cadres. The exclusion of Hitler's coalition partners (Hugenberg and Papen) from the Cabinet and the expansion of state and party agencies of repression (such as the Gestapo and the SD) all contributed to weaken the position of the military elite. It was all the more difficult for the military to resist because at the same time the basis for the realisation of its own *foreign policy* goals seemed to be much improved. Hitler had apparently succeeded in integrating the nation. General von Fritsch is said to have observed later in a mood of resignation that Hitler had succeeded in 'nationalising' the working class and thus in winning for a — supposedly — 'national' politics that large social group which even in Wilhelmine Germany had remained impervious to the influence of the military elite.[43] Similarly, Hitler appeared able to guarantee the nation's optimum preparation for mechanised industrial warfare by total mobilisation of the nation's resources.

Although the military elite believed that the conditions for solving the two central problems of its historical existence had improved, its own political position had in fact been substantially eroded.

V

Seen in terms of the categories of continuity and discontinuity, a fourth thesis can be formulated about the position of the military elite.

In historical perspective it was not 1933 but 1938 which proved to be the decisive break in the relationship between the military and politics in Germany. Despite altercations between representatives of the party and the military and despite the increasingly totalitarian character of the regime there had been until then a clear continuity in the political demands of the military elite.

The leadership of the armed forces, and especially the army command, despite their differences over tactics and methods, still claimed — in line with the traditional self-image of the Prusso-German military — to be a politically autonomous factor within the state, a force which participated in the decision-making process and thus had a share in executive power. Under the new regime this claim was embodied in the 'two-pillar theory' already mentioned, which suggested that the armed forces formed, alongside the party, one of the two elements which constituted the new system. After Hindenburg's death in summer 1934 Hitler arrogated his functions, among them the supreme command of the armed forces, which brought with it the problematic personal oath to the 'Führer and Reich Chancellor'. This certainly brought about a shift in the balance of power in so far as Hitler no longer represented only one 'pillar'. So much was openly acknowledged by some military personnel, among them the Chief of the General Staff, Beck.[44] But comfort could still be found in the admittedly contentious analogy with the *former* bearer of the crown during the time of the monarchy. Just as the Kaiser, representing the highest authority in the state, had once bridged the separate spheres of political and military power to ensure their unity in the Wilhelmine Reich, so Hitler, as Hindenburg's successor, would be able to fulfil the same function.

In the spring of 1938, however, Hitler did away with the last vestiges, institutional and in personnel, of traditional Prusso-German dualism. He removed the War Minister and the commander-in-chief of the army, together with a large number of generals, from their posts and from active service in what came to be known as the Blomberg-Fritsch crisis. A few months later he banished the chief of the army general staff, General Beck, to the wilderness. In this way the personnel who embodied the army's political perspective and its traditional view of itself were eliminated.[45] The institutions which embodied these perspectives were emasculated too in 1938, when Hitler assumed direct supreme command of the armed forces. From then on he exercised control by using the supreme command of the armed forces as his personal military staff – his 'Maison militaire' – and by granting his immediate subordinate, the Chief of the Supreme Command of the

Armed Forces, many of the functions of the Minister of Defence. From that point it was impossible for the military elite, bereft of representatives at the top, to play an independent, politically meaningful role even as an institution. The break in the historical development of the dualist principle of Prusso-German military history is evident.

The efforts of Beck as chief of the general staff to secure a fundamental change in the structure of the military leadership and in the responsibilities of the supreme military command (he made a number of attempts before 1938 and again during the Fritsch-Blomberg crisis) were not only a symptom of the permanent state of conflict typical of the Nazi regime. Nor was it merely a struggle over the guiding role in organising the nation for total war, a 'question fundamental to developed industrialised warfare' (Geyer). It was all that, certainly, but in the last analysis it was also an attempt by the military to realise a definite political concept of itself. For this reason the resignation and then dismissal of Beck, who had always been a prominent champion of the claim to political leadership, was symbolic of the developing discontinuity in the historical evolution of the Prusso-German armed forces. The new military leaders made this discontinuity evident in a number of ways.

The leading figures of both the army and the armed forces supreme command now had neither the will nor the ability to represent or apply the concept of an independent role for the army in the state. They no longer aspired to participate in fundamental decision-making or consequently in the power of the state. They confined themselves strictly to professional military matters and to executive functions on the instructions of the head of state and supreme commander of the armed forces – Hitler – who alone issued political directives and assumed responsiblity, and who had become their immediate, highest superior.

Their behaviour demonstrated the total defeat of the notion that in forming a coalition with the Hitler movement the military elite was creating for itself a broader base among the people. Hitler and his party had solved the problem of integration for their own ends and at the expense of the traditional elites. Men had reached the highest positions in the military hierarchy who no longer embodied the claim to a political role but who saw in Hitler's state, albeit to differing degrees, some of them not without reservation, the best possible basis of national organisation in an age of mechanised industrial warfare.

A schematisation of the complexities of individual standpoints and motivating factors can be formulated as follows. Those who were steeped in a tradition of political leadership by the Prusso-German military elite had believed that in forming a coalition with a nationalist populist mass movement they would find, under a restored dualism, a new legitimising base for their claim to a political role. It had failed. They were replaced by men who saw themselves only as a professional military elite within a nationalistic and totalitarian system of integration and who saw their first duty in the task of overcoming the problems of preparing for and waging modern mechanised industrial warfare.[46]

There are lines of continuity which bind even these representatives of the military with certain Prusso-German traditions. The decisive influences lie in the goals of foreign and domestic policy. The realisation of an essential element in the projected goal of domestic policy, a state structured along authoritarian lines, made the sacrifice of a specifically political role easier. At the same time the object of foreign policy, that of attaining a position of hegemony for the Reich in Europe, continued to be pursued singlemindedly in league with Hitler and under his command. Without doubt it was on this point that the military leadership of the time identified most strongly with the National Socialists.

Hitler's new lieutenants at the level of the command of the armed forces, above all Generals Keitel and Jodl, were enthusiastic supporters of the charismatic leader. They saw themselves exclusively in the role of loyal and committed instruments of their master's will.[47] Only the Führer, they believed, could release the energies of the people and the state in the way which was called for if the great aim was to be achieved: hegemony in Europe for a Greater Germany.

The new men in the army command, Colonel-General (subsequently Field Marshal) von Brauchitsch and his chief of the general staff, General Halder, consciously confined themselves to limited functions.[48] They made no claim to an independent role of any kind for the army. They were, however, determined to repulse as far as possible any interference by the party in military matters. In the end, of course, their determination was in vain.

Halder, chief of the general staff, hovered intermittently between thoughts of a *coup d'état* to prevent a war which might endanger the Reich's existence and brilliantly planning and executing Hitler's Blitzkrieg campaigns.[49] Although he recognised more clearly than his commander-in-chief the destructive and criminal character of the system and of Hitler's policies, he was unable to break out of the institutional and political mould which determined his actions. Nor, it seems, could he escape the lure of hegemonic and imperialist objectives, for the realisation of which Hitler's concept of the Blitzkrieg seemed most appropriate.

These high-ranking officers no longer constituted a traditional power elite struggling to preserve as much of their political position as they could. Their attitude was more that of a traditional leadership which overtly recognised that it could no longer survive independently because it had long lost the national power base it felt to be essential if it was to cope with secular problems of mechanised industrial warfare. But they still had the option of retaining an important position as a functional elite which was, for the time being at least, irreplaceable. They accepted this role more or less consciously; but the military command no longer had political aspirations of its own. The army leaders still exercised command as a functional elite acting in the name of the Führer and on his orders. But when they tried to assert themselves as a political force they were bound to fail. Even the failure of the abortive *coup* of 20 July 1944 had its roots in these circumstances. Stauffenberg and Beck wanted to restore in one liberating overthrow the old position of the military as a politically independent elite. But the military machine no longer responded unquestioningly to directives and orders with political implications. Their orders issued on 20 July seemed of dubious validity to some of the recipients, who refused to obey. As a functional elite this military leadership was in principle exchangeable. That much had been demonstrated at the climax of the crisis of winter 1941–42, when Hitler himself assumed command of all land forces and undertook a not inconsiderable revision of senior positions in the army in the east.

This fundamental abdication of political leadership can also be seen in the fact that the men of the supreme armed forces command like Keitel and Jodl, as also the army command under Brauchitsch, shared with organs of the state, and even with the party, wide areas of responsibility that were not of direct military concern in the realm of national defence and the conduct of war, such as the war economy. Almost as a matter of course, final co-ordination was left to Hitler. By presiding over the 'standing group' of the Reich Defence Council in 1933–34 Beck had still represented a claim to control all areas, even civilian and official party spheres, of importance for the defence of the nation in an era in which war affected the whole of society. After 1938 the representatives of the military command gradually ceded even classic military functions to other authorities, for example in more or less voluntarily accepting limitation of their executive power in the occupied territories, which passed largely into the hands of the party and the SS.[51] In armaments, events followed a similar pattern: there were occasions when military, civilian and party authorities coexisted in chaos, and times when they were in competition with one another. This was not merely an inevitable development of modern warfare. Although it may have been typical of Nazi rule, it was also an indication that the military elite had resigned its claim to overall leadership. The fact that the functional military elite was essentially replaceable was ultimately demonstrated within its own profess-ional sphere in 1944 when the Reichsführer SS was promoted to commander-in-chief of the home army and later for a time even to commander-in-chief of army groups, and when the new 'people's infantry divisions', the army reserve and the military secret service were placed under his command.[52] In a way this was a belated victory for the 'political, revolutionary warrior' who had not had a chance after 1918. Because of the collapse of Hitler's Reich the phenomenon was only temporary.

Within the framework of German military history the process we have outlined whereby what had once been a *political* elite was transformed into a merely *functional* elite can be termed 'revolu-tionary' in the sense that it brought about a fundamental break with historical tradition. In the Third Reich the Prusso-German officer corps became for the first time a purely executive agent of the state under political control. Such would certainly be its normal role under a liberal democratic constitution, whatever one might add as regards problems of the business state and the garrison state.[53] But this 'normality' had never existed in the Prusso-German empire or in the Weimar Republic. Prusso-German dualism had remained the hallmark of relations between the politicised armed forces and civilian politics throughout the changes of the time. At first glance it seems a paradox of history, that it should have been the Führer of a totalitarian regime who effected such a transformation in the relationship between the two forces as to correspond with liberal democratic constitutional principles. One could scarcely claim that constitutional normality had been achieved, however. It was rather a case of a bringing to heel of a totalitarian subjugation, to which the traditional military elite succumbed in its co-operation and collaboration with the leader of the National Socialist mass movement. The profound changes that had been wrought in the state, in society and in the economy from the onset of industrialisation, through the world war and the great inflation, up to the international economic crisis, may well have paved the way for this radical change in the history of the Prusso-German military elite, but they had not brought it about on their own.

Once he had achieved power it became possible for Hitler to establish an effective counterweight to the old leadership elites by virtue of the gravitational pull of his mass movement and the occasional consolidation of his rule by plebiscite. The old leadership elites were to a large extent mentally paralysed in their reaction by the apparent ability of Hitler's regime to enable them to realise their political aims at home and abroad; with eyes fixed on the supposed identity of their objectives they were blind to the fact that this identity was at best only partial and that Hitler's wider aims were inevitably destructive not only of their position but also of the state itself. The expectation of the military elite that, in alliance with Hitler, they could regain their lost power base among the people and solve long-standing problems of integration and mobilisation was bound to be disappointed. In fact the opposite occurred. Hitler represented for many Germans, at least for a time, the great alternative to traditional class society. He seemed able to fulfil the political and social desires of a large part of a nation that had been led for so long by entrenched power elites. He was capable, it seemed, of bringing about effective equality in the face of traditional privilege, and setting free the dynamic forces of modernisation, while at the same time offering protection against the frustrating consequences of that modernisation as well as securing property and authority.[54] In the face of these expectations, held by wide sections of the population, and the faith reposed in the promises of the Nazi regime, the old leadership elites did not have a chance, even if the expectation and the faith turned out to be a dreadful illusion.

VI

A *fifth thesis* can be formulated within the historical framework
already outlined: all the more important confrontations with the
party and its organisations can, for the most part, be interpreted as
efforts to prevent or even reverse this 'revolutionary' process.[55]
They were attempts to maintain or restore the *entente* character
which the regime had presented in 1933. They were attempts not to
let the foreign policy objectives be endangered by a course that was
perceived to be fraught with risk. They were attempts not to
jeopardise, or even forcibly to accentuate, the prerequisites of
national defence and counter-attack in the era of mechanised
industrial warfare, as seen by the military as a political and
professional elite. Only after a certain point, namely when Hitler,
and not just the party, its organisations or the·radical elements of
the Nazi movement, was recognised as the cause of the danger, did
these attempts take on a quality which can be characterised as
fundamental opposition. This recognition, however, occurred only
among that relatively small group of military men who, consciously
or unconsciously, still considered themselves a political elite or who
came to share such an understanding through confrontation with
the National Socialist system — those, in other words, who refused
to accept the reduction to a purely functional role. Because they
saw themselves as a political elite there were limits to co-operation
and collaboration beyond which opposition began.

Despite their individual criticisms the majority of the more senior
members of the officer corps, the personnel of which changed
radically in the course of the army's expansion, particulary during
the war, were not adversely affected in their accommodation to
Hitler and his regime. This accommodation was apparently broad
enough to assure the regime of the loyalty of the military leadership, even after its claim to an independent political role in the
state had been frustrated. From a historical point of view, this
loyalty on the part of a majority, on the basis of sufficient
consensus, and opposition by a minority, can be seen as two sides
of the same coin — that is, as two different reactions, on the part of
a traditional elite, determined by different motivating factors,
reactions to a combination of new and fundamental challenges in a
situation which was becoming ever more critical.

Different emphases and priorities within the military command

can be discerned here. The political claim of the military elite was
the essential and decisive factor for those officers who moved
gradually to a position of partial or ultimately even total opposition
to Hitler and his regime. On the other hand those representatives of
the military who resigned themselves to the position of a functional
elite saw the crucial factors as foreign policy objectives and the
preparation of the whole of society for war.[56] The ambition to
secure for the Reich hegemony in Europe, and even the status of a
world power,[57] together with the extensive militarisation of the
nation in the age of mechanised industrial war were, for them, the
important elements in the fundamental consensus of the senior
officer corps with Hitler and all he stood for. Evidently the aim of
hegemony, let alone that of world domination, and the conception
of great-power status were suitable compensation for the loss of a
position of power in domestic politics. At all events, the unswerving
loyalty of high-ranking officers can hardly be explained in full by an
attitude governed simply by a narrow professional outlook. In the
latter half of the war it was eventually recognised that certain
functional positions of leadership, the maintenance of German
power and the preservation of the regime had become inextricably
linked. This consensus held when Hitler inaugurated the campaign
against the Soviet Union as a war of annihilation. The politically
impotent military elite followed him, seeing in this eastern policy
both the resumption of earlier eastern and military policy dating
from the first world war and an ideological struggle to the death
against an enemy which was supposed to have been behind the
revolutions of 1918. The internal loss of power could thus be
compensated for in foreign policy and, indirectly, in ideology. But
as a result the military leadership was, in Andreas Hillgruber's
words, 'for the most part indirectly, but in some cases directly,
drawn into responsibility for the singular war of extermination
which Hitler, casting aside all the canons of the laws of war,
conducted on the territory of the Soviet Union.'[58] So it was that the
army came to be undeniably implicated in Hitler's programme of
genocide. What made it possible was partly the moral weakness
and willingness to be led of the upper echelons, partly the growing
affinity among officers and men with Nazi ideology and Hitler's
foreign policy, but not least a justified fear of the consequences if
they refused to obey orders.[59] Such complicity conclusively sealed
the fate, politically and historically of the military elite.

Summing up, it can be said that the defeat of Hitler's Reich involved a traditional military elite's failure to preserve, by means of *entente* with the Nazi movement, its special position, social and political, through the profound political, ideological and socio-economic changes of the twentieth century and in that way to meet at the same time the political and professional challenge posed by mechanised, industrial warfare.

The attempt destroyed the traditional elites once and for all, and contributed to the destruction of the German nation state and the division of the old Europe.

Notes

1 Cf. the critical bibliographical accounts by Michael Geyer, 'Die Geschichte des deutschen Militärs von 1860 bis 1945. Ein Bericht über die Forschungslage (1945 bis 1975)', in *Die moderne deutsche Geschichte in der internationalen Forschung*, edited by Hans-Ulrich Wehler (Geschichte und Gesellschaft, No. 4. 1978), pp. 256–86, and *id.*, 'Die Wehrmacht der Deutschen Republik ist die Reichswehr. Bemerkungen zur neueren Literatur', *Militärgeschichtliche Mitteilungen*, XIV, 1973, pp. 152–99. See also the comprehensive bibliographical data in the *Handbuch zur deutschen Militärgeschichte*, published by the Militärgeschichtliches Forschungsamt and edited by Othmar Hackl and Manfred Messerschmidt, Munich, 1975. – In what follows reference will be made only to the literature which is the most important within the limits set by the line of argument. Cf. also the articles by Volker R. Berghahn, 'Militär, industrialisierte Kriegführung und Nationalismus', *Neue Politische Literatur*, 26, 1981, pp. 20–41; Stig Förster, 'Der deutsche Militarismus im Zeitalter des totalen Krieges', *ibid.*, 27, 1982, pp. 133–46; and Stig Förster, 'Von der Marne zu Euroshima', *ibid.*, 29, 1984, pp. 443–52.
2 *Documents Diplomatiques Français*, Series 1, V, document No. 195 of 4 January 1934.
3 Bundesarchiv-Militärarchiv, N28/2; cf. Müller, *Heer und Hitler*, p. 233 f.
4 On military memoirs see G. Breit, *Das Staats – und Gesellschaftsbild deutscher Generale beider Weltkriege im Spiegel ihrer Memoiren*, Boppard, 1973 (Wehrwissenschaftliche Forschungen, Part 1: Militärgeschichtliche Studien, 17).
5 Hermann Foertsch, *Schuld und Verhängnis. Die Fritsch-Krise im Frühjahr 1938 als Wendepunkt in der Geschichte der national-sozialistischen Zeit*, Stuttgart, 1951; John Wheeler-Bennett, *The Nemesis of Power: the German Army in Politics, 1918–1945*, London and New York, 1956; Siegfried Westphal, *Heer in Fesseln. Aus den Papieren des Stabschefs von Rommel, Kesselring und Rundstedt*, Bonn, 1950; Adolf Heusinger, *Befehl im Widerstreit. Schicksalsjahre*

der deutschen Armee 1923–1945, Tübingen and Stuttgart, 1950; Walter Görlitz (ed.), *Generalfeldmarschall Keitel, Verbrecher oder Offizier? Erinnerungen, Briefe, Dokumente des Chefs OKW*, Göttingen, Berlin and Frankfurt a. M., 1961; cf. from a later period Curt Siewert, *Schuldig? Die Generale unter Hitler. Stellung und Einfluss der hohen militärischen Führer im nationalsozialistischen Staat. Das Mass ihrer Verantwortung und Schuld*, Bad Nauheim, 1968. On foreign writing, which in the 1950s very largely determined the discussion of the question of the German army and politics, see above all the report, full of ideas, by Hans Herzfeld, 'Zur neueren Literatur über das Heeresproblem in der deutschen Geschichte', *Vierteljahrshefte für Zeitgeschichte*, IV, 1956, pp. 361–86, and *id.*, 'Das deutsche Heer als geschichtliches Problem,' *Zeitschrift für Politik*, I, 1954 and *id.*, *Das Problem des deutschen Heeres 1918–1945*, Laupheim, 1952.

6 Cf. Manfred Messerschmidt, 'Werden und Prägung des deutschen Offizierkorps', in *Offiziere im Bild von Dokumenten aus drei Jahrhunderten*, Stuttgart, 1964 and Karl Demeter, *Das deutsche Offizierkorps in Gesellschaft und Staat 1650–1945*, Frankfurt a. M., 4th edn., 1965.

7 Geyer, 'Geschichte des deutschen Militärs', p. 266, with reference to the earlier work of B. L. W. Munca, *The Junker in the Prussian Administration under William II, 1888–1914*, New York, 2nd edn., 1970, alludes correctly to the fact that not only the social structure should be considered here but *a fortiori* the problem of a traditional power elite in a rapidly changing socio-economic milieu.

8 On this interpretation of the structure of the Prusso-German Wilhelmine Reich compare Hans-Ulrich Wehler, *Das deutsche Kaiserreich 1871–1919*, Göttingen, 1973, and the important reviews of this book by Thomas Nipperdey, 'Wehlers "Kaiserreich". Eine kritische Auseinandersetzung', *Geschichte und Gesellschaft*, I, 1975, pp. 539–60, and by Hans-Günter Zmarzlik, 'Das Kaiserreich in neuer Sicht?', *Historische Zeitschrift*, CCXXII, 1976, pp. 105–26. Wehler's reply is to be found in *Historische Zeitschrift*, CCXXV, 1977, pp. 347–8. Recently David Blackbourn has maintained that the feudal elites too opened themselves to bourgeois attitudes. On this process of what is called 'the aristocratic bourgeoisification' cf. D. Blackbourn, *Class, Religion and Local Politics in Wilhelmine Germany*, Wiesbaden, 1980.

9 On this point and the following see Theodor Schieder, *Das deutsche Kaiserreich von 1871 als Nationalstaat*, Cologne and Opladen, 1961; Hans-Ulrich Wehler, *Krisenherde des Kaiserreichs 1871–1918. Studien zur deutschen Sozial- und Verfassungsgeschichte*, Cologne, 1970. For further literature see Wehler, *Kaiserreich*. Another important work on this theme is Wolfgang Sauer, 'Das Problem des deutschen Nationalstaates', in *Probleme der Reichsgründungszeit 1848–1879*, ed. Helmuth Böhme, Cologne, 1968, pp. 448–79. On the debate on the Wilhelmine empire cf. David Blackbourn and Geoff Eley, *Mythen deutscher Geschichtsschreibung*, Frankfurt, 1980;

Geoff Eley, *Reshaping the German Right: Radical nationalism and
political change after Bismarck*, New Haven, 1978. Cf. also the
controversial debate between G. Eley and H. J. Puhle, H. U. Wehler
and H. A. Winkler in *Geschichte und Gesellschaft*, 4, 1978, and in
Merkur, 35, 1981.

10 On this point in general see the collections *Reichsgründung 1870/71.
Tatsachen, Kontroversen, Interpretationen*, ed. T. Schieder and Ernst
Deuerlein, Stuttgart, 1970, and *Das kaiserliche Deutschland. Politik
und Gesellschaft 1870–1918*, ed. Michael Stürmer, Düsseldorf,
1970, but more especially Wehler's book, *Kaiserreich*, and also Dirk
Stegmann, 'Zwischen Repressionen und Manipulation. Konservative
Machteliten und Arbeiter- und Angestelltenbewegung 1910–1918',
Archiv für Soz. Geschichte, XII, 1972, pp. 351–432. In *Krisenherde
des Kaiserreichs*, p. 137, Wehler points to the absence of 'a generally
binding basis of legitimation' in the Reich, which he attributes to the
'tradition of revolution from above'.

11 In addition to the literature cited in note 6 see M. Messerschmidt,
*Militär und Politik in der Bismarckzeit und im wilhelminischen Deut-
schland*, Darmstadt, 1975, (Erträge der Forschung, 43) and Martin
Kitchen, *The German Officer Corps, 1890–1914*, Oxford, 2nd edn.,
1973; on the navy see Holger H. Herwig, *The German Naval Officer
Corps: a Social and Political History 1890–1918*, Oxford, 1973. Cf.
also Bernd F. Schulte, *Die Deutsche Armee 1900–1914. Zwischen
Beharren und Verändern*, Düsseldorf, 1977; *id.*, *Europäische Krise
und Erster Weltkrieg. Beiträge zur Militärpolitik des Kaiserreiches
1871–1914*, Frankfurt, 1983, and Dennis E. Showalter, 'Army and
society in imperial Germany: the pains of modernization', *Journal of
Contemporary History*, vol. 18, 1983, p. 585–618.

12 The best summary of the literature on this question is M. Messer-
schmidt, *Militär und Politik*, pp. 32–54 and *id.*, 'Die politische
Geschichte der preussisch-deutschen Armee', in the *Handbuch zur
Militärgeschichte*, published by the Militärgeschichtliches Fors-
chungsamt and edited by O. Hackl and M. Messerschmidt, II,
Munich, 1975.

13 On this point see the standard works of M. Geyer, in particular,
besides his critical analysis of previous literature cited in note 1,
Aufrüstung oder Sicherheit, and 'Der zur Organisation erhobene
Burgfrieden', in K.-J. Müller and Eckardt Opitz (eds)., *Militär und
Militarismus im der Weimarer Republik*, Düsseldorf, 1978, pp.
15–100. In these studies Geyer develops a comprehensive interpretative frame of reference whose central elements are the ideas of
'industrialisation of warfare', 'delimitation of the (military) use of
force' and the 'socialisation of warfare' together with the 'socialisation of danger'. In my view Geyer's central idea of the 'industrialisation of war' attaches too little significance to the weight of the
continuing socio-political traditions of the Prusso-German state and
its officer corps. Moreover I feel that, beyond the phenomenon of
industrialisation, insufficient conceptual consideration has been

given to the very important element for the military of mechanisation. (On this point cf. Andreas Hillgruber, 'Kontinuität und Diskontinuität in der deutschen Aussenpolitik von Bismark zu Hitler', in *id.*, *Grossmachtpolitik und Militarismus*, p. 16.) I would therefore prefer the concept of the 'technological-industrial war' or 'mechanised industrial war'. For the historical dimension see especially Michael Howard, *War in European History*, London, Oxford and New York, 1976.

14 On this point see the literature cited in Geyer, 'Geschichte des deutschen Militärs', p. 258 ff.

15 This simultaneous, double challenge seems to me to be the decisive element in its development, and to stress the aspect of 'industrial warfare' alone is to pay it insufficient consideration.

16 Thus Geyer, 'Geschichte des deutschen Militärs', p. 283.

17 On this point see Bernd Wegner, *Hitlers politische Soldaten. Die Waffen-SS 1933–45*, 1982 (English translation Oxford, 1987), especially Part One; for the SA see the article by Richard Bessel, 'Militarismus im innenpolitischen Leben der Weimarer Republik. Von den Freikorps zur SA', in Müller and Opitz, *Militär und Militarismus*, pp. 193–222, which gives reference to further literature, and his recent book *Political Violence and the Rise of Nazism*, New Haven and London, 1984. Also important is the Ph.D. of E.P. Guth, 'Der Loyalitätskonflikt des deutschen Offizierkorps in der Revolution 1918–1920' (*Europäische Hochschulschriften*, Rh.III, Bd. 198), Frankfurt am Main, Bern and New York, 1983.

18 In assessing the military elite's conduct the claim to be a political elite *and* the reaction to the phenomenon of 'technological-industrial war' are to be seen in close connection. This is overlooked when attention is focused on 'industrial warfare' only. This objection could be levied against the otherwise fundamental work of M. Geyer (cf. notes 1 and 13 above). General von Seeckt's way of thinking shows the precise extent to which the claim to be a political elite *and* insight into the reality of modern warfare affecting the whole of society went hand in hand. In his memorandum of January 1921 on 'Fundamental Thoughts on the Rebuilding of the Armed Forces' (printed in Friedrich von Rabenau, *Seeckt – Aus seinem Leben 1918–1936*, Leipzig, 1940, p. 474 ff.) this officer, mostly seen as the embodiment of the traditionalist, politically elitist general staff officer, clearly recognised and put into words the phenomenon of warfare affecting the whole of society and the preparatory measures necessary for this, such as, for instance, the 'use of the nation's full military power' even in peace time, the commissioning of industry and the psychological 'tuning' of the population. I cannot discern a difference between an 'older, so to speak elitely conservative militarism' and a 'quasi-revolutionary militarism', as was manifest, for instance, in the contrasting pair of Seeckt – Schleicher/Reichenau. (On the other hand see A. Hillgruber, 'Militarismus am Ende der Weimarer Republik und im Dritten Reich', in *id .*, *Grossmachtpolitik und Militarismus*, especially p. 50.) On this

problem of 'the army in transition from the Wilhelmine Reich to the Republic' see in general the valuable collection of sources *Zwischen Revolution und Kapp-Putsch. Militär und Innenpolitik 1918–1920*, ed. Heinz Hürten, Düsseldorf, 1977 (Quellen zur Geschichte des Parlamentarismus und der politischen Parteien, series 2, II).

19   Cf. D. Bald, *Sozialgeschichte und Rekrutierung des deutschen Offizierkorps von Reichsgründung bis zur Gegenwart* (Schriftenreihe Innere Führung, Reihe Ausbildung und Bildung, 29), Munich, 1977, p. 24 ff, 30 ff and tables 1 and 6. There is reference to further literature in this book. The share of the sons of the former upper strata of society (officers, senior civil servants, landowners) rose to 88 per cent up to 1930, and if the sons of manufacturers and businessmen are included the figure was 92 per cent (*ibid.*, p. 32 and table 6). Cf. also Reinhard Stumpf, *Die Wehrmachtselite. Rang- und Herkunftsstruktur der deutschen Generale und Admirale*, Boppard, 1982. But see also Geyer's pertinent critical comments, 'Geschichte des deutschen Militärs', p. 266, 29, with regard to arguments supported solely by social statistics. It is interesting to note the parallel development in France after the defeat in 1940: R. O. Paxton, *Parades and Politics at Vichy: the French Officer Corps under Marshal Pétain*, Princeton, N.J., 1966, p. 414 ff, proved that the officer corps of the armistice army had a larger share of graduates from the Grandes Ecoles, in particular Saint-Cyr, which were rich in tradition, than the army of 1938. Reserve officers who had been called up again, officers from the ranks and Jewish and Masonic officers were systematically eliminated. This regression to a professional and politico-social elite is an interesting analogy to the 'Reichswehr'

20   F. Hossback, *Zwischen Wehrmacht und Hitler*, Wolfenbüttel, 1949, pp. 162–67, ascertains that, with the exception of two generals, all twenty-eight generals in the army's leading posts from 1934 to 1938 had gone through the world war on the general staff. Fifteen came from the nobility and thirteen were of middle-class origins.

21   The aim of restoring Germany's position as a great power had already been clearly expressed during the well known meeting of leading officers in the general staff on 20 December 1918 in Berlin, at which both Seeckt and Schleicher appeared as authoritative speakers: cf. the account in F. L. Carsten, *Reichswehr und Politik 1918–1933*, Cologne and Berlin, 1964, p. 25, and Rabenau, *Seeckt – Aus seinem Leben*, p. 117 ff. In general see also Hillgruber, *Kontinuität und Diskontinuität*, pp. 25–31, and F. Fischer, *Bündnis der Eliten*, especially chapter three, 'Tradition against democracy: the army and the tradition of the power state', p. 82 ff. Cf. too T. Nipperdey, '1933 und die Kontinuität der deutschen Geschichte,' *Historische Zeitschrift*, CCXXVII, 1978, pp. 86–111.

22   For Groener's directive: Bundesarchiv-Militärarchiv, PG 34072; cf. G. Post jr., *The Civil–Military Fabric of Weimar Foreign Policy*, Princeton, N.J., 1973, p. 196 ff, and Geyer, *Aufrüstung oder Sicherheit*, p. 215 ff. For Blomberg's directive: IMT XXXIV, docu-

ment 175–C; *cf. D. C. Watt, Too Serious a Business: European Armed Forces and the Approach to the Second World War*, Berkeley and Los Angeles, Cal., 1975, p. 107 ff, and K.-J. Müller, *General Beck*, chapter V.

23 Deist, 'Zum Problem der deutschen Aufrüstung', p. 549; id., 'Die Aufrüstung der Wehrmacht', in *Das deutsche Reich und der Zweite Weltkrieg*, Militärgeschichtliches Forschungsamt, Stuttgart, 1979, pp. 371–532; id., *The Wehrmacht and German Rearmament*, London, 1981.

24 Cf. K.-J. Müller, *General Beck als Generalstabschef*, chapters, IV and V, and the following study in the present volume.

25 Hans Meier-Welcker, *Seeckt*, Frankfurt a. M., 1967, in particular chapters X–XII and XVII; Carl Guske, *Das politische Denken des Generals von Seeckt. Ein Beitrag zur Diskussion des Verhältnisses Seeckt – Reichswehr – Republik*, Lübeck and Hamburg, 1971.

26 Cited in Thilo Vogelsang, 'Neue Dokumente zur Geschichte der Reichswehr 1930–1933', *Vierteljahrshefte für Zeitgeschichte*, II, 1954, p. 409.

27 Cited in Heinz Hürten, *Reichswehr und Ausnahmezustand. Ein Beitrag zur Verfassungsproblematik der Weimarer Republik in ihrem ersten Jahrfünft*, (Rheinisch-Westfälische Akademie der Wissenschaften, G222), Opladen, 1977, p. 47. There is an abbreviated version of the quotation in *Die Kabinette Marx I und II*, (Akten der Reichskanzlei. Weimarer Republik, ed. Karl Dietrich Erdmann and Hans Booms), ed. G. Abramowski, Boppard, 1973, p. 176 ff.

28 Cited in Carsten, *Reichswehr und Politik*, p. 336.

29 On this point and the following see the account in K.-J. Müller, *Das Heer und Hitler*, pp. 20–34.

30 Peter Bucher, *Der Reichswehrprozess. Der Hochverrat der Ulmer Reichswehroffiziere 1929/30*, Boppard, 1967 (Wehrwissenschaftliche Forschungen, Abteilung Militärgeschichtliche Studien, VI). The testimony of one of the participants: Richard Scheringer, *Das grosse Los unter Soldaten, Bauern und Rebellen*, Hamburg, 1959. Proof of the alternative idea mentioned can be seen from the fact that one of the three participants later became a high-ranking SA leader, while another joined the communists.

31 Cf. A. Hillgruber, 'Militarismus am Ende der Weimarer Republik und im "Dritten Reich"', in *id., Grossmachtpolitik und Militarismus*, p. 37 ff. See also T. Vogelsang, *Neue Dokumente*, and especially Karl Dietrich Bracher, Wolfgang Sauer and Gerhard Schulz, *Die nationalsozialistische Machtergreifung. Studien zur Entwicklung des totalitären Herrschaftssystems in Deutschland 1933–1934*, 2nd edn., Cologne and Opladen, 1962, and K. D. Bracher, *Die Auflösung der Weimarer Republik. Eine Studie zum Problem des Machtverfalls in der Demokratie*, 5th edn., Villingen, 1971; cf. likewise the dissertation by M. Geyer, *'Aufrüstung oder Sicherheit'*, and the one by J. R. Nowak, 'Kurt von Schleicher – Soldat zwischen den Fronten', Würzburg, 1969, and T. Vogelsang, *Reichswehr, Staat und NSDAP*,

Stuttgart, 1963, and *id.*, *Kurt von Schleicher*, Göttingen, 1965 (Persönlichkeit und Geschichte, 39). Cf. also Friedrich-Karl von Plehwe, *Reichskanzler Kurt von Schleicher*, Munich, 1983, and Axel Schildt, *Militärdiktatur mit Massenbasis? Die Querfront-Konzeption der Reichswehrführung unter General v. Schleicher am Ende der Weimarer Republik*, Frankfurt, 1981.

32 On this point and the following see Geyer, *Aufrüstung oder Sicherheit*, and Deist, 'Aufrüstung 1933–1936', p. 546 ff.

33 On the events surrounding the formation of the government and the armed forces' role: K.-J. Müller, *Das Heer und Hitler*, p. 35 ff. and W. Sauer, in Bracher, Sauer and Schulz, *Die nationalsozialistische Machtergreifung*, p. 685 ff.

34 On the 'twin pillar' theory: K.-J. Müller, *Das Heer und Hitler*, chapter II, and M. Messerschmidt, *Die Wehrmacht im NS-Staat*, chapters I and II, and the summary based on these two works in Michael Salewski, *Wehrmacht und Nationalsozialismus 1933–1939*, Munich, 1978 (Handbuch zur deutschen Militärgeschichte 1648–1939, IV).

35 The armed forces command's role in the consolidation of the regime has been thoroughly described in W. Sauer, 'Die Mobilmachung der Gewalt', in Bracher, Sauer and Schulz, *Die nationalsozialistische Machtergreifung*.

36 On this thesis and the following: K.-J. Müller, *Das Heer und Hitler*, chapters II–V. Similar findings, even if the emphasis is different, in M. Messerschmidt, *Die Wehrmacht im NS-Staat*, chapters II and III.

37 Hossbach, *Zwischen Wehrmacht und Hitler*, p. 104.

38 On Reichenau see K.-J. Müller, *Das Heer und Hitler*, p. 53 ff, which also has the quotes, and the memoirs of his former colleagues: Edgar Röhricht, *Pflicht und Gewissen. Erinnerungen eines deutschen Generals 1932–1944*, Stuttgart, 1965, and Smilo von Lüttwitz, *Soldat in vier Armeen*, Part One (unpublished, to be found in Bundesarchiv-Militärarchiv, N10/9).

39 Cf. K.-J. Müller, *Das Heer und Hitler*, p. 78 ff, and M. Messerschmidt, *Die Wehrmacht im NS-Staat*, p. 40 ff. See the summary in Salewski, *Wehrmacht und Nationalsozialismus*, section B.3c, p. 56 ff.

40 Röhricht, *Pflicht und Gewissen*, p. 42 ff. Cf. also Field Marshal Erich von Manstein, *Aus einem Soldatenleben 1887–1939*, 4th edn, Bonn, 1963, p. 275: 'Concern over basic questions of loss of political liberties such as freedom of speech has far less significance for the armed services.'

41 The decrees are printed in *Offiziere im Bild von Dokumenten*, documents Nos. 101 (Blomberg), 103 (Weichs); on the interpretation see K.-J. Müller, *Das Heer und Hitler*, p. 192 ff, and, with a different emphasis, M. Messerschmidt, *Die Wehrmacht im NS-Staat*, pp. 58 ff, 79 ff. The following quotes by Reichenau (discussion of 25 November 1935) to be found in Bundesarchiv-Militärarchiv, WK VII/1343.

42 Reported in the unpublished memoirs of General Smilo von Lüttwitz, *Soldat in vier Armeen*, Part One (Bundesarchiv-Militärarchiv, N10/9).

43 Foertsch, *Schuld und Verhängnis*, p. 205. How widespread and continuous the feeling was that an integration of those social groups could no longer be guaranteed singlehanded and by means of their own instruments of power can be seen from General von Reichenau's statements of 1933/34 cited in noted 38 above and the much earlier comment in the diaries of the Adjutant to the last Prussian Minister of Defence, Captain Gustav Böhm, who noted on 8 November 1918 that the ideas and hopes of the masses could 'not be shot down by guns' (*Adjutant im Preussischen Kriegsministerium. Juni 1918 bis Oktober 1919. Aufzeichnungen des Hauptmanns Gustav Böhm*, ed. Heinz Hürten and Georg Meyer, Stuttgart, 1977, p. 57 (Beiträge zur Militär – und Kriegsgeschichte, 19)). 44. See the following study in the present volume on General Beck, in particular his attempt to balance the shifts in power by prompting General Ludendorff to take political action. It seems that the fatal oath to Hitler was instigated by General von Reichenau out of calculated political considerations, to bind Hitler for his part closer to the armed forces: cf. K.-J. Müller, *Das Heer und Hitler*, p. 135 ff.

45 On the Fritsch-Blomberg crisis see Harold C. Deutsch, *Hitler and his Generals: the Hidden Crisis, January–June 1938*, Minneapolis and London, 1974, and the relevant chapter in K.-J. Müller, *Das Heer und Hitler*. On Beck's resignation see both the following study and K.-J. Müller, *General Ludwig Beck*, chapter VI.

46 It was the claim to be a political elite which divided the two groups within the military elite. There were often severe differences of principle on this question, in particular between Beck and Keitel. On the other hand, as far as the requirements of 'technological industrial warfare' were concerned there was broad agreement: Keitel had called in 1932 within the Organisation Department of the General Staff for the 'total commissioning of the individual for military purposes', according to the analysis of the corresponding document in Geyer, 'Burgfrieden', p. 85; about a year later Beck, in his capacity as chairman of the standing group of the Reich Defence Council, had argued that there was 'scarcely a practical undertaking in public life which is not of importance for the Reich's defence'; use must therefore be made of every opportunity of action even in times of peace (Eighth meeting of the Standing Group: Bundesarchiv-Militärarchiv, Wi I F 5/701).

47 On Keitel, Görlitz (ed.), *Verbrecher oder Offizier*; on Jodl, Luise Jodl, *Jenseits des Endes. Leben und Sterben des Generaloberst Alfred Jodl*, Vienna, Munich and Zurich, 1976. There is an analysis of Keitel and Jodl's attitudes and opinions in K.-J. Müller, *Das Heer und Hitler*, *passim*, in particular p. 231 ff.

48 On Brauchitsch, K.-J. Müller, *Das Heer und Hitler*, p. 262 ff, and Messerschmidt, *Die Wehrmacht im NS-Staat*, chapters IV and V.

49 On Halder, K.-J. Müller, *Das Heer und Hitler*, *passim*, and Harold C. Deutsch, *The Conspiracy against Hitler in the Twilight War*, London and Minneapolis, 1968; also the critical records of his former

subordinate: Helmuth Groscurth, *Tagebücher eines Abwehroffiziers 1938–1940, mit weiteren Dokumenten zur Militäropposition gegen Hitler*, ed. Helmut Krausnick and H. C. Deutsch, Stuttgart, 1970 (Quellen und Darstellungen zur Zeitgeschichte, 19); from an apologistic point of view there is Gräfin Schall-Riaucour, *Aufstand und Gehorsam. Offizierstum und Generalstab im Umbruch. Leben und Wirken von Generaloberst Franz Halder, Generalstabschef 1938–1942*, Wiesbaden, 1972.

50 Peter Hoffman, *Widerstand, Staatsstreich, Attentat. Der Kampf der Opposition gegen Hitler*, Munich, 1979, in particular chapter XI, and *id.*, 'Zum Ablauf des 20. Juli 1944 in den Wehrkreisen', *Wehrwissenschaftliche Rundschau*, XIV, 1964, pp. 377–97, and *id.*, 'Der 20. Juli im Wehrkreis II (Stettin): Ein Beispiel für den Ablauf des Staatsstreichversuches im Reich', *Aus Politik und Zeitgeschichte. Beilage zur Wochenzeitung "Das Parlament"*, 14 July 1965, pp. 25–37.

51 For the beginnings of this development see H. Umbreit, *Deutsche Militärverwaltung 1938/39. Die militärische Besetzung der Tschechoslowakei und Polens*, Stuttgart, 1977.

52 Heinz Höhne, *Der Orden unter dem Totenkopf, Die Geschichte der SS*, Gütersloh, 1967.

53 Harold D. Lasswell, 'The Garrison State', *The American Journal of Sociology*, XXXXVI, 1941; *id.*, 'The Garrison State hypothesis today', in S. P. Huntington (ed.), *Changing Patterns of Military Politics*, New York, 1962. See also A. Lüdtke, 'Militärstaat und Festungspraxis', in Volker R. Berghahn (ed.), *Militarismus*, Cologne, 1975 (Neue Wissenschaftliche Bibliothek, 83).

54 David Schoenbaum, *Hitler's Social Revolution*, New York, 1966, 1968, and in a similar vein Ralf Dahrendorf, *Gesellschaft und Demokratie in Deutschland*, Munich, 1971. This question has recently been treated from a specific viewpoint in a work rich in both substance and thought: Timothy W. Mason, *Arbeiterklasse und Volksgemeinschaft. Dokumente und Materialien zur deutschen Arbeiterpolitik 1936–1939*, Opladen, 1975.

55 On this subject see the two other studies in the present volume.

56 On this point reference is again made to Colonel-General Beck and Field Marshal Keitel as the (so to speak) archetypal representatives of these different views: Beck, the representative of the claim to be a political elite in its purest and most demanding form, and Keitel, who consciously only wanted to be the executive organ of the Führer. See his closing remarks at the Nuremberg trial: *Keitel, Verbrecher oder Offizier*, p. 385 ff, when he referred to 'obedience and loyalty' and 'a soldier fulfilling his duty'. On the other hand, Beck spoke in a note in a lecture of 16 July 1938 (Bundesarchiv-Militärarchiv, N 28/4) of the fact that a soldier in the highest post had to see his duties and tasks not merely 'within the limited framework of his military orders'. However, precisely because both groups of officers of whom we have labelled Beck and Keitel representative were at one over the necessity

of a total organisation of the nation in the age of 'technological industrial warfare' (see note 46 above) this distinguishing factor, either a 'political' or a 'functional' elite, the tradition of the Prusso-German military elite, receives such an essential function in an historical interpretation.

57 On the still controversial problem of the (continental or global) objective of Nazi foreign policy see the collection by Wolfgang Michalka (ed.), *Nationalsozialistische Aussenpolitik*, (Wege der Forschung, 297), Darmstadt, 1978.

58 A. Hillgruber, 'Militarismus am Ende der Weimarer Republik und im "Dritten Reich"', in *id.*, *Grossmachtpolitik und Militarismus*, p. 49 ff.

59 Thus Helmut Krausnick and Hans H. Wilhelm, *Die Truppe des Weltanschauungskrieges. Die Einsatzgruppen der Sicherheitspolizei und des SD 1938–1942*, Stuttgart, 1981, p. 278.

Colonel-General Ludwig Beck, Chief of the General Staff, 1933–38

Some reflections and the results of recent research[1]

I

Ulrich von Hassell once called Ludwig Beck the 'centre' of the resistance.[2] Without doubt, the chief of the general staff, who resigned in 1938 in protest against Hitler's war policy, was one of the central figures in the national conservative opposition movement. In speeches, commemorative articles and descriptive portrayals intended for a general reading public, as also in the historical literature, which has only recently shown a critical approach to research into the opposition to Hitler, his name is always cited along with Goerdeler's and Stauffenberg's and, not unjustly, it heads the list. In ethical and intellectual qualities he overshadowed all other military figures in the resistance.

In these circumstances it is at first glance surprising that there is still no scholarly biography, despite the numerous references and mentions Beck has received. This remains true despite the fact that in addition to some biographical sketches three accounts of the general's life have been published.[3]

It is just as surprising, even if to a degree understandable, that there is still no academically adequate account of the man's professional activity as Chief of the General Staff, as the military leader who, along with the commander-in-chief of the army, General von Fritsch, can be called the creator of the new army. This can perhaps be attributed to the specific form and manner in which the question of 'the military and the Nazi regime' has long been handled in Germany. Not only have resistance on the one hand and collaboration, if not complicity, on the other, always been carefully kept as two distinct concepts, they have also been considered in strict isolation from each other. No correlation has been adduced between these complexes so arbitrarily separated, nor have historical phenomena been examined from the viewpoint of the two issues simultaneously.[4] This has led to considerable distortion and to a discernible narrowing of outlook not conducive to a comprehensive understanding or a discriminating assessment of the people and issues involved.

Ludwig Beck has to a certain extent fallen victim to this particularist approach. Up to now the literature on him has, if we disregard details, been governed basically by two tendencies.[5] In the first place it has been determined by a view preoccupied by the resistance, that is to say by an attempt to draw as full a portrait as possible of Beck-the-resistor, to depict him as a protagonist of the opposition and of the resistance within Germany from the outset. Accordingly there has been a tendency to view the whole of his activity, his political ideas, his patterns of behaviour almost solely from the standpoint of his role in the resistance. This has come about in a largely determinist way, as if his personal, mental and political development necessarily carried him inevitably into opposition. The particular perspective which has long influenced the public and also, largely, the academic treatment of the German resistance in the Federal Republic further promoted this tendency. On the other hand it was difficult at first to make the phenomenon of a German opposition known and comprehensible to the reluctant victors, who were committed to the thesis of collective guilt, and to a less open-minded German public, the majority of whom had at least for a while come to an accommodation with the Nazi regime. On the other hand 'well-meaning authorities', understandably enough, cultivated the remembrance of the opposition not least to give the new German republic moral legitimacy, a sort of *raison d'être*. The situation was equally favourable to enthusiastic apologising and unreflective heroising.

This tendency to interpret in an unthinking, heroising fashion can be seen in the treatment of Beck's personality from the standpoint of preoccupation with the resistance movement. This standpoint is also at the bottom of the second tendency which has characterised his treatment by academics and journalists alike: a perspective, found in many interpretations, strongly determined by the politics of the present day.

Examples of these two specific approaches are easy to find in the literature on Beck. It is typical of the first tendency mentioned above that practically everything Beck did or said in his official capacity that could bear a critical interpretation has been seen exclusively from the point of view of the resistance. Professional activities of the Chief of the General Staff which in themselves had nothing whatsoever to do with opposition let alone resistance have been fitted into this one-sided view of the resistance.

A typical example is the interpretation of Beck's well known memorandum of 20 May 1934, arguing against too rapid a build-up of the army.[6] In the literature it is overwhelmingly regarded as the earliest voice of responsible military policy raised against Hitler's headlong rearmament. Nothing could be further from the truth. Rather, from December 1933 Beck had energetically and repeatedly demanded speedy and extensive rearmament. In the summer of 1934, by the autumn of that year at the latest, he was all for introducing universal conscription. He even contested Hitler's designation of a total of only twenty-one divisions as the rearmament target of the Reich government after Germany had left the Disarmament Conference and the League of Nations. Highly critical, he observed to the Reich Chancellor that all of thirty-six divisions should have been called for, and equipped with heavy armament to boot. Increasing the size of the army by degrees would only give the Versailles powers repeated grounds for protest. The memorandum of 20 May 1934 was not, therefore, aimed at Hitler's supposedly over-hasty rearmament plans and demands at all . It was directed instead against the General Army Office (Allgemeines Heeres-Amt, or AHA), one of the offices in the army command which had long assumed the mantle of critic and rival to the General Staff (Troop Office). In his dispute with the AHA Beck was not concerned with the volume or tempo of rearmament but solely with arrangements for it.

Should all twenty-one planned divisons be drawn up immediately as skeleton formations which were then to be developed only slowly into combat-ready bodies of troops? Or should the approach be more cautious, with existing combat-ready units kept in a majority to begin with, and then gradually building up additional new divisions, so that large, combat-ready forces were always on hand? The latter alternative seemed sensible to Beck, not just in view of the reactions to German rearmament expected from abroad but also in the light of the power struggle with the SA.[7] Beck wanted to keep powerful units at the ready so as to be in a position to resist the SA's military, political and social revolutionary intentions. Seen in the light of this aspect of domestic policy, the controversy with the AHA as reflected in the famous memorandum of 20 May[8] was thus an internal dispute within the army and not an argument with Hitler over his rearmament policy. It was a technical, military debate about the strategy of rearmament and it has, therefore, nothing whatsoever to do with any political opposition, whatever its nature, to the Führer's aim of rearming at full speed.

The myth propagated by General Speidel and other writers is representative of the second trend in interpretation, namely that governed by present-day political preconceptions. According to this legend Beck was a pioneer of Franco-German reconciliation and amity. He is portrayed as one who stood for peaceful compromise between two nations which were 'sworn foes' and almost as a herald of the policy of reconciliation with France initiated under Adenauer. His journey to France in the summer of 1937 is interpreted as the manifestation of a species of policy of European reconciliation and solidarity.[9]

In this regard Schramm, one of his biographers, even maintains that Beck had become firmly convinced of the necessity of Franco-German *détente* since his time as a lieutenant in Alsace-Lorraine before 1914.[10] Nothing could be more incorrect. Neither the actual early history of the incident nor the sources on it, which are well known, allow such an assessment of the Paris visit. To begin with it can be firmly stated that the journey did not in any sense take place at Beck's instigation or as a result of any independent initiative on his part. It was not a spectacular gesture by the Chief of the General Staff. This is clear from the circumstances leading up to the visit.[11] General Gamelin had met the Defence Minister, von Blomberg, in London on the occasion of the funeral of King George V, and invited him to Paris. Gamelin's motive was undoubtedly to further a relaxation of tension through such contacts. Blomberg hedged, but said that he would send Beck. That was at the beginning of 1936, but the idea of a visit was not reactivated until over a year later. Even then the initiator was not Beck but the German military attaché in Paris, General von Kühlenthal, who urged Beck in several letters in pay a visit. He wrote to the Chief of the General Staff, 'I consider such a visit beneficial and important. *Quite independently of how German policy is going to develop some day, we soldiers are, in my opinion, interested in having peace for a few years'*. At first Beck was not particularly enthusiastic. Indeed, he seemed hesitant. When he finally went, however, it was with the explicit approval of the Minister and of the Foreign Office, which had briefed him beforehand on the state of German-French relations. Beck's trip to Paris in the summer of 1937, outwardly represented as a private visit to the World Exhibition, was therefore not an act of personal initiative on the part of the Chief of the General Staff with the possible intention of making peace more secure in the shadow of an aggressive regime in Germany. It was intended rather to help ease tension in military and foreign affairs with a view to distracting attention politically from Germany's massive unilateral rearmament, the tempo and scale of which threatened at that time to destabilise the posture of affairs in Europe. At the end of 1936 Beck had put in motion the decision to set up a motorised and armoured offensive army. Until the build-up was complete Germany urgently needed good relations with her neighbours, a period of *détente* to enable her to complete the rearmament without interruption from foreign interference.

The interpretation of the visit as prompted by the notion of a German-French *rapprochement*, as an individual intitiative committed to the peaceful cohesion of Europe as a whole, by a responsible soldier, directly counter to his government's policy, is a typical instance of the politically motivated representation of historical facts. It emerged at a time when Franco-German reconciliation and German rearmament were the central elements of Konrad Adenauer's policy. Members of the German General Staff who, as commanding officers in the federal army, the Bundeswehr, had a say in German military policy at the time probably saw in such an interpretation an opportunity to furnish the former General Staff with a kind of retrospective alibi. They did so by suggesting a line of continuity from Beck to Adenauer.[12] Available sources do not, however, substantiate such an interpretation. On the contrary, all the General's known statements on this subject show a consistently cool and reserved, if not entirely hostile, attitude to the Reich's western neighbour until well into the war.[13] In a letter of 28 November 1918, written with the impression of the military collapse and the armistice fresh in mind, he wrote, 'The French at least recognise only one fact: revenge, revenge, and again revenge, and whoever expects anything else from them is a fool . . . France wants to crush Germany. That is my firm belief, based on a long acquaintance with the national character.' Evidence from a later period also shows that Beck regarded France as one of his country's main enemies both before and after his journey to Paris in 1937. 'It certainly seems to me that every question we pose on the subject of the military and military policy can be seen only within the framework of relations with France, and not in its own right. France will always remain on the opposing side, our harshest and strongest enemy,' he wrote in spring 1934. Scarcely a year after his trip to Paris, in a variation on this theme, he stated, 'It is true that France will always stand in the way of any extension of Germany's power and in this regard will always be seen as Germany's certain enemy'.

These remarks appeared in a statement on Hitler's comments to leading representatives of the government and the armed forces of 28 May 1938. However much he rejected Hitler's short and medium-term foreign-policy plans, in his statement he agreed almost entirely with Hitler's assessment of France. Evidence from the years 1941–42 confirms that Beck held to this view even during the war.[14] There is no mention of a German-French settlement or even of Franco-German friendship in the ideas on Europe that emerge in the memorandum 'The objective' which was at least partly inspired by him. The exact opposite is the case. Contrary to the widely accepted interpretation mentioned, it must be affirmed unequivocally that the sources available to us show that Beck saw France as a sworn enemy of any German aspiration to great-power status. They bear no sign of a German–French compromise. Beck saw the relationship between France and Germany solely in terms of power and rivalry.[15]

II

Where does the critical analysis of such interpretations lead? It is clear that interpretations based primarily on political consider-ations are both factually and heuristically inadequate, if not downright dubious. But an interpretation which persists in adop-ting a perspective focused entirely upon resistance is also one-sided and therefore not sufficient to enable us to appreciate Beck's historical significance. His influence must be examined from other points of view. What points of view could these be?

In the first place one must be aware that Beck has to be seen primarily as what he was at first: Chief of the General Staff, the leading military figure who, alongside the commander-in-chief, was responsible for the army's organisation, training and strategic or operational planning. As such his character and official activity should nevertheless be seen within a broader framework. He must be regarded as one of the representatives of the Reich's traditional ruling elite whose *rapprochement* and co-operation with the leadership of the Nazi movement in 1933 constituted the Third Reich. However much the motivation and behaviour of those who offered it may have differed in detail, their multifarious assistance was important in shaping the first phase of the Hitler regime. Such a perspective would be necessary merely to understand Beck's role in the resistance, if one took the view that the later opposition and subsequent resistance of national-conservative circles developed in many respects from a sort of negative reaction to their earlier co-operation with the representatives of National Socialism. In this sense, but of course only in this sense, the national-conservative resistance was an extreme, complementary phenomenon to the entente and co-operation with Hitler on the part of the traditional elites. Consequently the study and elucidation of particular characteristics of the national–conservative opposition belongs within the larger context of the whole phenomenon of co-operation by leading social and political groups with the Nazis. Beck's evolution from the new German army's Chief of General Staff to central personality in the resistance should likewise be seen within the framework of this entente between two very unequal power groups.

It is clear from these considerations that within such an interpretative framework Beck's activities can no longer be seen, or at least no longer seen exclusively, from the category of 'resistance'. Only the principles of his political thought and his political values can offer suitable criteria for assessing his behaviour in a broader context.

What was the categorical framework in which his political ideas were formed?

Analysis of his theoretical writings and his official memoranda in the light of this question reveals that his thought and behaviour were determined by two fundamental ideas which were rooted deep in the tradition of the Prusso-German military state.[16]

The first is that of the army's special role and position in the state and in politics. In his view the army — and that naturally meant the officer corps — ought to have an independent position distinct from all other institutions of the state. This was a traditional concept in Prussian thought.

The second was a consequence of the first: that the military as an institution must share in the power in the state, that is, in the making of essential policy decisions. This obtained not only for issues of military policy and strategy but also for foreign and large areas of domestic policy. On the one hand it was a manifestation of hallowed Prussian tradition, but on the other it also reflected Beck's conception of the requirements of modern warfare.

For Beck the premise that war was a political phenomenon and that, accordingly, 'politics' was the decisive factor, in no way meant that the politician or statesman should have primacy. Rather, he drew the opposite conclusion. A responsible supreme military commander should be active at a political level, sharing in decision-making and the responsibilities of government precisely because war is a political phenomenon. This argument and the conclusions that follow are to be found in numerous phrases and considered statements in Beck's writings. In 1938 he wrote in his study 'The commander at war'[17] that the participation of the military high command was necessary in all questions of foreign policy which concerned war or the prospect of war, that is, in all questions of power politics.

In this necessary 'participation in foreign policy by the presumptive commander-in-chief' Beck in no sense envisaged the commander-in-chief in the role of technical adviser on such questions as the efficiency and preparedness for action of a limited instrument of executive power for achieving any given political ends, plans or concepts — to be consulted by the statesman just as the departments of finance or economics, for example, might provide the ruling politicians with assistance in arriving at decisions. Doubtless many of his statements reveal that he set the statesman and the commander-in-chief on the same level as part of a team and thought they should work closely together. The very words he uses make this evident. He speaks of the supreme military commander 'controlling the instrument of war'. He characterises the co-operation between politician and military supremo as an 'exchange of ideas'. He draws a picture of two luminaries of equal weight and importance by citing Seeckt, 'The statesman asks the commander-in-chief, What can you do? What can the others do? And the commander-in-chief replies with a question: What do you

want? What do the others want?' The view of both luminaries as
equal can be seen too in Beck's claim, expanding on Seeckt's ideas
that under certain circumstances it is the commander-in-chief's
right and duty to resist the politician's demands.

With regard to the military commander's sphere of influence
Beck ultimately goes even beyond the realm of foreign policy and
power politics. This again indicates that he perceived the supreme
commander as more than the mere representative of a department
of state whose sphere of influence and participation is, by nature of
his position, only slightly greater than that of other executive
departments. In an essay of 1938 he wrote that it was 'the right and
the duty of the art of war to extend its strategic deliberations to the
area of politics', in the sense, that is, of politics as the comprehensive, transcendant sphere of activity, outlined above. Going into
detail he points out that owing to the political nature of war the
military command must also be involved whenever questions of
domestic policy, public administration, food supply, the economy
or the nation's 'inner steadfastness' are to be decided. Two years
later he repeated all this in his 'Observations on war' (1940), where
he observes, 'The scope and the responsibilities of the supreme
strategist [can] . . . not be drawn too wide'. Beck thus elevates the
supreme military commander to the all-encompassing 'political'
sphere. In this construction the politician and the military commander function together in the realm which Beck calls 'politics'. The
concept of the 'primacy of politics' does not refer to the 'politician'
or the 'political leadership' but to the level at which the two men
who bear highest responsibility, one in military and the other in
civil affairs, act in principle together, albeit in different ways.

But how might power be distributed in this political area of
common interest between the soldier and the politician? Do they
stand side by side as equals or does Beck differentiate gradations in
the rights and responsibilities of the one and the other?[18]

In itself Beck's ideal, like Clausewitz's, is the union in one person
of both functions. But, like Clausewitz, he is conscious that his ideal
model is no longer realistic, given the growing complexity of the
situtation and the way in which the political structure has changed.
Consequently the 'dualism of the statesman and the commander-in-
chief' is for him 'a reality we have to make the best of'. He imagines
the co-operation between the two as basically an equal pairing of
the statesman and the highest-ranking military officer. He therefore

dissociates himself both from Bismarck's thesis that the politician must keep the upper hand in the conduct of war and the opposite view of Moltke, that the military command in wartime should act completely independently of the civil power. He regards neither view as 'incontestable on all counts'. Referring to Clausewitz's theory of the relationship between 'war and politics' Beck repeatedly stresses that the statesman and the commander-in-chief belong closely together. They must 'use their intellect to plan together'; they have to work constantly together in a relationship of trust. He therefore places them on an equal footing.

The blueprint for a War Cabinet which he drew up in 1938 is characteristic of Beck's view.[19] In this draft 'the commander at war', the generalissimo, takes his place next to the 'head of state', who would take the chair. The deputy head of state is the highest-ranking military officer, not the Foreign Minister, for instance, who is the only representative of civilian authority still in the Cabinet. 'Thus the commander at war is in the last analysis the decisive figure,' writes Beck, especially as the head of state in his role as supreme commander takes pains not to 'descend from the high watch tower of the supreme military command'. The superiority of the military component is underlined by the fact that the commanders of the three constituent forces, the army, navy and the air force, are represented as standing members of the War Cabinet while the civilian heads of the Ministries of economics, food and finance do not have permanent seats, as still less do departments of secondary importance, in the event of war. They are to be consulted only occasionally, like the Under Secretary for Military Affairs and the Propaganda Minister, as 'temporary members'. In contrast Beck demands that the military commander-in-chief be granted participation in the leadership 'in the areas of domestic administration, food supply, the war economy, including finance, and the morale of the civilian population'. In certain circumstances the War Cabinet itself ought to be totally excluded from the deliberations and decision-making of the Premier and the commander-in-chief.

Behind this view of the military's relationship to politics lies a dualist conception of the state: a view of the state resting on the twin pillars of 'politics', or rather the political leadership, and the 'military'. A more detailed analysis than is possible here would confirm that the model of the state at the root of Beck's ideas on the military and their relation to politics was that of a supra-individual, authoritarian structure translated into an idealised realm far removed from the real world, and essentially bearing the hallmark of the dualism of political civilian and military power. This dualism, as we know, was characteristic of the Prusso-German state before 1918 and constituted one of its most onerous structural burdens.[20]

In accordance with this dualistic interpretation of the state Beck claimed for the army leadership a share in power on the strength of the special constitutive value of the armed forces in the state. Participation in power meant participation in government decision-making, not only in foreign but in domestic policy as well.

The claim to extensive participation by the military in certain areas of the domestic affairs of the nation was founded on two factors. Historically it derived from the traditions of the militarised state of Prussia, the traditions of a political system 'which does not have an army but is an army that has a state', to recall the well-known remark of a foreign observer in the eighteenth century. Secondly, however, Beck's claim reflected a more recent development, the trend towards total war which had emerged since the industrialisation of war and the means of waging it.[21] Beck concluded from the experience of 1914–18 that the tendency must inevitably be for the preparation and conduct of war to engage the whole of a country's resources. His dualist concept of the state, according to which the heads of the civil and military powers had to act in unison, was therefore an appropriate model. His ideas united Prussian tradition and the modern image of warfare.[22] The breaking down of the divisions separating the bourgeois civilian sphere from the professional military one as a consequence of total war between modern industrialised states, which had also blurred the dividing line between armed conflict and stages of peace, formed the legitimising foundation of this understanding of the state as of the tradition of the old Prussian military state.

In accordance with his conception of this ideal, and as a result of supposedly compelling historical necessity, an almost ideal situation seemed in Beck's eyes to have become reality in 1933: the party (under Hitler's leadership) and the army command, united under the field-marshal's presidency, seemed to be the formative powers in the new Reich. Beck's interpretation of the state as founded on tradition and necessity makes his welcome of the government formed in 1933 understandable. In a private letter of March 1933 on 'the political revolution' he wrote, 'I have hoped for it for years and am glad that my expectation has not proved false. It is the first great ray of hope since 1918.'[23]

At that time, in a speech which received particular attention from the army's leaders, Hitler referred to the new state of the 'Third Reich' as based on twin pillars, the party and the army.[24] The correspondence with Beck's own conception of the political ideal was exact. But this apparently programmatic declaration by the National Socialist Führer was not the only thing that seemed to confirm for Beck that his imagined ideal was about to be realised. At the end of the year, shortly after his appointment to Chief of the Troop Office, that is, of the general staff, as in reality it was, he was appointed chairman of the Executive Committee of the National Defence Council. Its task was to prepare in peacetime for the mobilisation of the entire nation in the event of war, under the supervision and direction of the military command. Entirely in line with Beck's ideas, this meant that in the overall distribution of responsibilities the military command was superior to all other departments of state. Beck's ideal structure could scarcely have been better or more perfectly realised, at least in intent.

III

Beck's evolution from opposition, ultimately the side of resistance, was no straight path. For long periods it was characterised by attempts to give the regime, or to preserve for it, the character which the General, in keeping with his conceptions of the ideal, believed lay at the heart of Hitler's state, or, rather, which he wished to prevail under the purported entente between National Socialism and the traditional elites. His road into opposition thus began inevitably with his progressive *disillusionment* about the chances of seeing his own ideal state, realised.

In the last analysis arguments about principles and conceptions of the ideal, their preservation or enactment, lay at the root of the major conflicts Beck was involved in during his time as Chief of the General Staff. The conflicts all developed within the framework of his interpretation of the state, his understanding of politics and his conception of the necessary role of the army within the state. For a certain period of time it was not a matter of pursuing activities which aimed at the overthrow of the system. It was a question not of fundamental opposition but rather of applying or preserving those principles which, springing from Prussian tradition and the imperatives of modern industrialised warfare, governed his actions in the realms of politics, military policy and, equally important, in the sphere of military professionalism, something so far over-looked. It was not the case that his movement towards a stance of opposition and his professional work as Chief of the General Staff, as co-founder of the new army, were unrelated and distinct. Instead there was an indissoluble bond between the two. Many occasions of conflict, seen in retrospect — that is, from the perspective of 20 July 1944 — appear as early manifestations of resistance, but they were in fact above all else essentially either disagreements of a purely military, professional nature or arguments over the preservation of a system about which Beck nursed quite definite ideas. Occasionally they were both at one and the same time.

This led among other things to the fatal situation where particular decisions on military policy which Beck made on professional military grounds tended to hamper his freedom of action *vis-à-vis* the regime rather than assist it. Such was the case with his military-political activity, and, above all, with the re-equipment of the army, which was chiefly conceived and brought to realisation by him.

Take for example, his long-running argument with the Armed Forces Command about the shape of the supreme military leadership structure, and about the supreme military command's relation to the political leadership. Here we can see the extent to which Beck regarded a question which seems at first glance no more than a technical one of organisation as an essentially political problem, and dealt with it according to the assumptions fundamental to his political beliefs and his conception of the state. In the last analysis the attempt to bring his ideal vision of a dualist state to reality was at the root of the heated arguments which pervaded almost his whole period of office as Chief of the General Staff.[25]

On Beck's part, it was less a technical question of organisation, than an attempt to secure for the supreme military authority a participatory role in the responsibilities and decision-making processes of government. His demand that the area of activity and responsibility of the highest military representative must include the relevant political spheres proves that for him it was a question of bringing to fruition this principle of a dualist structure. The principle may well have been adapted to the new realities of the Nazi dictatorship but in substance it remained unchanged.

He was constantly putting forward new proposals designed to give the general staff and the high command the function, which seemed to him necessary and sensible, of an advisory and co-determining body in key concerns affecting the military and military policy as well as foreign policy. According to one army command memorandum inspired by Beck the commander-in-chief was no mere obeyer of orders, like a common grenadier; he adhered unswervingly to the requirement that the army leadership — that is, the commander-in-chief and the Chief of the General Staff, had to be the head of state's sole advisers on questions of strategy and military policy, and thus in all matters of vital importance to the nation. The profound and highly political nature of this conflict was clearly recognised by Beck's opponents in the supreme armed forces command. At that time, in contrast to Beck, Generals Keitel and Jodl represented the 'primacy of politics' in the sense of the absolute superiority of the politically accountable statesman over the military commander. Jodl correctly identified Beck's position when he wrote that the army's general staff, 'ensnared by memories of an earlier day, feels responsible for political decisions instead of obeying and fulfilling its military imperatives'. In complete contrast to Beck's view these two officers regarded the military, and with it the highest representatives of the army, exclusively as an instrument of the political leadership. To be sure, Keitel's and Jodl's perception of the primacy of politics did not stem from assumptions of liberal constitutional thought, according to which the military, as part of the state executive, had an instrumental character. Their attitude was based on the National Socialist 'leadership principle', which they sought to apply in the relationship of the military to politics. Keitel was later to explain at Nuremberg that he had represented 'the leadership principle in the military field', because 'according to the National Socialist idea, the Führer alone was entitled to make the decisions'. For men like these the army was an instrument of the Nazi leader's power.[26]

Beck took exactly the opposite view: the army and its leadership were a constituent part of the state pure and simple. Here we see the implacable collision of the 'leadership principle' with the 'twin pillar theory', a thesis Hitler adopted for purposes of propaganda and manipulation but which Beck regarded as the classic formula of his perception of the state. For the men in the Armed Forces Command, in whose favour Hitler finally decided in 1938, the military was part of the executive, part of the Führer's power. They reproached Beck and the general staff with being a bastion of outmoded tradition, that Prussian tradition of military and political dualism at the highest level of the state. Beck, on the other hand, held fast to his view that the military command had a more than merely technical right to advise; it had a right to share in political debate and political responsibility as well. In accordance with Prussian tradition, and with Hitler's 'twin pillar theory' and, not least, with the requirements of modern warfare, the army must have a privileged position in the state.

Initially Beck attempted, in complete conformity with the regime, to shape the state and the position of the military command within it according to his own perceived ideals and along the lines which it was supposed were intended by Hitler. He even imposed the arrangement against internal resistance. The complex issues cited above, however, make it clear how it was possible for his efforts to lead in the long run to reaction, opposition and ultimately resistance on his own part as he came to realise more and more the fundamental incompatibility of his own ideal with the reality.

This point was not, however, arrived at until relatively late. At first, convinced of the regime's fundamental suitability and concordance with his perceptions of the ideal, Beck tried at many levels and in many different areas to transmute this perception into reality, or rather to avert any threat to it. In this regard reference should be made to a little known episode, mentioned in the literature either not at all or else inaccurately, which reveals its fundamental importance when viewed in connection with his political aspirations and beliefs.[27]

In 1935–36 Beck had had discreet and intensive contacts with General Ludendorff. Until now it has been supposed that they were connected with efforts by the army command to repair the shattered relationship between Ludendorff and Hitler on the occasion of the General's approaching seventieth birthday.[28] But if the sources are read more closely and in the light of his political principles another picture emerges.

Beck at that time wanted to induce General Ludendorff to co-operate with the army politically. In Beck's opinion and in that of other high-ranking officers the army had lost ground after Hindenburg's death in 1934. The balance of power appeared to have shifted towards the party. The political consequences had already become apparent. From the end of 1934 on, acute tensions had several times arisen between the army and certain forces in the Nazi movement. The weighty reproach that the army was not loyal to the regime and was politically unreliable loomed large in these conflicts. Beck saw in them not an expression of the Nazi movement's claim to total power but only the work of 'radical elements' which Hitler had nothing to do with.

That was the situation during the period when Beck made contacts of a highly political nature with Ludendorff which stretched over a year and a half. Beck sought to make the best-known wartime general the political spokesman of the army's interests, as a successor, so to speak, to the deceased field-marshal and President, Hindenburg, at a time when tension was high, the future uncertain and a power struggle loomed between the army and sections of the party. Ludendorff's intervention, that is, his political reactivation on the army's behalf, was intended to forestall any redistribution of power in the vacuum that followed the death of Hindenburg when the army's relationship with the party seemed liable to slip. In this way the entente character, the 'twin pillar' construction might be stabilised. The high regard in which Beck held Ludendorff's political and moral influence at the time can be seen in an observation he made after his resignation in 1938. 'Since Ludendorff's death Hitler has faced no more impediments [*vis-à-vis* the army] . . . He [Ludendorff] was the only one he [Hitler] still respected,' he said.[29]

But at a time when Beck was urging Ludendorff's intervention in a manner which was scarcely short of conspiratorial, he was acting less against Hitler than against those factions within the party which he repeatedly labelled 'radical elements' and which sought to dispute the army's right to its position in the state. The political background to Beck's initiatives is attested by one of Ludendorff's closest collaborators, who acted as intermediary in these contacts: 'Already in 1934–36 Fritsch and Beck . . . were trying to take the only practical way at that time of changing the Nazi regime. They intended to make use for the benefit of the armed forces of the one man for whom Hitler still had some respect.' Holzmann's word is confirmed by contemporary sources. At the time Ludendorff said in a letter that he declined to take part in this game, as it would have meant being 'drawn into responsibility without power'. Moreover the General's wife wrote to her husband's political agent in Berlin after one of Beck's visits, 'See that my husband does not get involved. The services are only going to make use of him.'[30] When Ludendorff consistently refused to respond to Beck's advances the latter finally broke off contact.

This politically explosive episode contributes to the elucidation of Beck's relationship to the Third Reich. He was neither a determined opponent of the regime from the outset, nor was he an uncritical adherent of National Socialism . The incident confirms rather that for Beck the model on which the new state was based was entente between the traditional leadership elites, in particular the military elite, and the head of the Nazi movement. The classic definition of this entente was to be found in the twin pillar theory.

Moreover the Ludendorff affair confirms Beck's readiness to act resolutely and energetically whenever the army's position in the state, and thus, in his eyes, in the whole structure of the regime, was endangered. In 1934 the conflict with the SA had already made that clear when, with the commander-in-chief, General von Fritsch, he put sections of the army on alert and prepared some combat units for action against the SA if necessary. At the time this task was spared them by the SS's murderous attack. In another context Beck's resolution was also revealed by the Ludendorff affair in that he attempted to secure the army's political position by activating such a prominent figure.

At the very time when, after all the nightmare experiences with the SA and other 'radical' groups in the Nazi movement, the foundations of the state as he comprehended it appeared exposed to chronic threat, when with Hindenburg's death a decisive safeguard was removed, he acted in accordance with his beliefs to secure the army's position *politically*. He was also prepared to enforce it against sections of the Nazi movement, if necessary, indicating a degree of vigour, even *vis-à-vis* the Führer himself. On the other hand that did not yet mean attacking Hitler and the regime; on the contrary, he wanted to restore the regime to accordance with its original ideals. Hence his actions were not direct or immediate but rather indirect, as the negotiations with Ludendorff demonstrate. That is to say, they were pursued in a critical situation by rearranging the pieces in the political jigsaw, by introducing into the game a new political force, be it real or only supposed.

All this still does not prove any fundamental opposition to the regime itself. Many of the General's critical statements from these years have indeed been preserved but they all reflect the distinction, already mentioned, between a well-meaning Führer and untrustworthy 'radical elements' in the party. He said to a confidant in mid-1935 that Hitler really stood above all acts of spite. At that time he saw the Führer in an entirely favourable light; this gave Ludendorff cause to remark in critical vein that Beck's credulity was hair-raising.

The Chief of the General Staff was apparently under the impression at that stage that Hitler himself had to hold his own against the disastrous influence of these 'radical' elements. They threatened the army's position in Hitler's state and thus, in Beck's eyes, the system itself. He nursed the imagined distinction between Hitler and the 'radical' elements of the movement for some time. Later he was again to see them at work, this time in foreign policy. In 1937 he observed critically that certain elements in the party — he named Himmler, Goebbels, Heydrich and Rosenberg — might press the Führer to deflect attention from the regime's internal problems with initiatives in foreign policy. He strongly denounced the irresponsibility of any such moves. In his eyes the 'radical' forces would not only endanger the security of the Reich with hazardous foreign adventures but would also encroach on areas which, from Beck's perspective, were the preserve of the supreme military and political leadership. When Hitler made it clear that he was not inclined to consult, on strategy and tactics in the game of power politics, the leaders of the army in that partnership based on trust which Beck regarded as the ideal form of co-operation between the military and politics, but instead, as in 1938, he began of his own volition to pave the way for an armed assault on Czechoslovakia, then in Beck's eyes the Führer himself had offended against one of the crucial principles of the Third Reich, the 'twin pillar' theory, and had thus jeopardised the entente character of the regime. But it was precisely at this moment that the fateful consequences of Beck's professional competence were to be seen. His work on military and rearmament policy had in the meantime set dates and created realities which made it more difficult than ever for him to counteract the course events were taking.

IV

For a long time Beck's military policy, or rather its principal component, rearmament policy, has been treated only incidentally in the literature, when not entirely neglected, even though it was the central element of his professional activities. If one ignores the question of the tank force, the study of this area has been almost totally eclipsed by the almost exclusive concentration on the issue of resistance. Not only has the General's professional work, building up the new army of universal conscription to form the basis of the armed forces in wartime, been disregarded, but an avenue essential to understanding his course in opposition has also been blocked. Recent years have seen the beginnings of research, based on voluminous official source material, into the complex issue of German rearmament policy and, with it, Beck's military achievement and influence.[32] In this regard it is nevertheless also true that his military and rearmament policy can be understood adequately only if the world of his political ideas, in particular his concept of foreign policy and power politics, and his vision of the imperatives of warfare between industrialised countries, are included as interpretative categories.

Beck's rearmament policy is certainly misunderstood if, following the apologists, one stresses his wish to rearm solely for purposes of defence and to safeguard the security of the Reich, in contrast to Hitler's rush to rearm from motives of aggression against the will of the Chief of the General Staff. This view is, as the evidence reveals, incorrect. An analysis of Beck's concept of foreign policy and of his actual rearmament policy[33] disproves such undifferentiated views. What follows is a very brief outline.

Without question the ideal of a position for Germany as a great European power lay at the heart of his understanding of foreign policy objectives. For a high-ranking officer whose view of the world had been decisively moulded by the mighty Wilhelmine Reich, imbued with the spirit of Empire, that is not, after all, surprising. It is, however, surprising that such an assessment has not previously been inferred from the evidence available.

What was Beck's perception of this aim of establishing Germany as a great power? Did it, in the General's case, remain within the limits of attempting to revise her position as a nation state — in the sense, for example, of largely or completely freeing her from the provisions of the Treaty of Versailles? Or did his conception of Germany as a great power encompass imperial, hegemonic aspects, such as, for example, a vision of a Central Europe deprived of political power?

It was this question which indirectly lay behind a controversy which sought to ascertain, as part of the larger objective of analysing the motivation of the national-conservative resistance, whether, as Trevor-Roper sees it, the imperialist extension of Hitler's policies beyond nation-state revisionism drove the national-conservative opposition to action, or whether, as Graml sees it, the paths of Hitler and his national-conservative coalition partners had already divided when the dictator proceeded to seek change by warlike means.[34] The literature is almost universally agreed that it was Hitler's violent methods, heedless of the risk of war, and not the imperialist overstepping of nation-state aspirations that first drove the Chief of the General Staff into opposition and ultimately into resistance.[35] In this context we can adduce his flat refusal in May 1935, combined with a threat of resignation, to prepare a feasibility study for an operation against Czechoslovakia 'suddenly, like a surprise attack'. Two years later, despite instructions from the Minister of Defence, he did no work on a study of Special Operation Otto — a military intervention in Austria in the event of a restoration of the Hapsburgs – as a protest. Beck's rejection of armed force in the pursuit of nation-state revisionist claims reached its climax with his 'struggle against war' in the Sudeten crisis of 1938. The struggle led him to thoughts of a *coup d'état* and ultimately ended with his resignation.

All this appears correct when the evidence is examined from the standpoint of his growing inclination to resistance. If the same sources are examined in the light of the question formulated above, however, they give much more complex answers. From the viewpoint of the origins of his drift to resistance, certain passages in his notes and memoranda recede into the background, or the full force of what they state is not correctly perceived. The problem of 'war or peace?' has been drawn into the limelight by this tendency to see Beck from the resistance point of view, and it has totally eclipsed the question of political aims, which in his opinion were to be pursued peacefully, or at least without too great a risk of war. It has also, equally significantly, not allowed the question of the functional value which is to be attributed to his rearmament policy to be discussed at all.

For Beck the central point of reference was and always remained the idea of Germany as a great power. In his view this idea was fundamentally opposed and challenged by other countries. As an objective it was of such profound and unquestioned importance to him that a deeper or more critical reflection on the role and position of a great power in the European concert of nations and its relations to other states of the first or second rank is nowhere to be found among his notes. For him the magnitude of the objective was self-evident.

Can Beck's vision of Germany as a great power and the possibilities considered for realising it be described more closely from the sources available? As far as a policy of revision of the nation-state is concerned, a detailed study of his position on the Austrian question provides some indications from which significant provisional findings can be drawn in the endeavour to throw more light on his views about foreign policy.

The interpretation of his attitudes to the Austrian question[36] has in the past occasionally been the cause of difficulty. Initially, in 1937, Beck had energetically warned against thoughts of military intervention in the event of a restoration of the Hapsburgs, which would, of course, have made a union of the two countries impossible. As already mentioned he firmly refused to carry out any such planning exercise. In the first place he considered the office which had made the request, that is, the Armed Forces Office, as lacking in jurisdiction and professionally incompetent. His refusal was aimed in the first instance at the authority which had saddled him with a task which had not been adequately thought through.

Secondly, as regards the annexation of Austria itself, he did not reject it in essence, only at that particular time, because certain prerequisites of foreign policy and power politics had not been met. German intervention would bring, in addition to France, other powers into the arena — Czechoslovakia, at all events — and could therefore not be isolated. The international situation simply did not allow of such an enterprise. A military blueprint ought not to leave the overall international position out of consideration. As a third counter-argument Beck claimed that the Austrian army would certainly offer resistance. This would mean that the 'future relationship between Germany and Austria' would 'be based not on their union, but on the rape of Austria'. For him it was, therefore, in this case a matter of establishing Germany's status as a great power in agreement with the Austrians. He was against any kind of action which would jeopardise such agreement. Fourthly, and equally important, was his reference in the memorandum to the fact that 'Germany . . . in regard to her army [is] *not yet* in a position to provoke the risk of a war in Central Europe'. From this it is clear that Beck thought that revision of the Versailles arrangements — the first condition of Germany attaining any sort of position as a great power — was achievable by means of the weight of German arms; and in theory that that might well not exclude another modern 'war to found the Reich' in Central Europe. But it was important for him that every step should be carefully calculated, should be commensurate with the country's resources and should remain in tune with actual international power relations. This was military politics aimed at securing great-power status but it was more cautious, cleverer and better thought out than the great-power politics of Wilhelmine Germany.

The goal of establishing Germany as a great power was to be striven for by means of classic power politics, which included an element of military power. But at the same time international games of chance and a policy of risk were to be excluded. Such a line of thought, however, could not help but fall quickly into a fundamental dilemma. Such power politics presumed military pressure, or at least the availability of the means of military pressure, and yet, on the other hand, it tied the realisation of its objectives to optimal international conditions. One must question, therefore, whether, in view of the balance of power and the relationships between the countries of Europe at that time, extremely narrow limits were set for a peaceful settlement, and whether a policy of military pressure had not inevitably to give rise to opposing forces: even carefully calculated great-power politics could thus soon end in deadlock. Was this type of great-power politics, based on military back-up, and going beyond the point where a peaceful settlement was no longer practicable, still feasible in Central Europe? Did not Beck's proviso that the overall international situation had to permit of such an undertaking also imply the probability that the realisation of great-power status for Germany would have to be deferred to a utopian future? Strictly speaking, given the general situation of Europe at the time, such a proviso could only lose its basic importance if it obtained solely for a transition period, after which the resort to armed force from a position of strength which had been won in the meantime was not excluded. Was this the sense of the passage cited above? The answer requires an examination of the rearmament policy Beck pursued.

First, however, let us return to the question of whether Beck's vision of Germany as a great power might not have gone beyond the level of the nation-state and had an imperialist bias. An analysis of his attitude during the Sudetenland crisis provides the initial basis of an answer.

If we disregard the question of Hitler's motives, the Sudeten affair is generally seen as involving a non-German state some parts of which nonetheless lay fundamentally within the scope of aspirations to national unification. Yet it was at least equally a problem of preserving or changing the existing power structure in Europe. It was universally recognised at the time that severing the Sudetenland from Czechoslovakia would, in military, strategic and political terms, reduce Czechoslovakia's importance in Europe to such an extent that she would be drawn irretrievably into the gravitational pull of the German Reich. Just such a development occurred as a result of the Munich conference. Czechoslovakia's downfall, therefore, meant the first if not the decisive step in Germany's rise to the status of a major Central European power of at least potentially hegemonic status.

What view did Ludwig Beck, Chief of the General Staff, take of these considerations? Did he regard the Sudetenland as a legitimate object of national revisionist aspirations or did he perceive the problem in the light of its importance for the power structure of Europe as well? Did he see in fact both these sides of the Sudetenland issue? Such a question figures only very obliquely, if at all, in the detailed attention the subject has received in the literature hitherto. In keeping with the view which emphasises resistance, his struggle against Hitler's chancy policy of armed force is highlighted as the beginning of his own open opposition. Because of the prevailing interest in his arguments against Hitler's Sudeten adventure the full import of Beck's key comments on the Czechoslovakian issue has not been sufficiently heeded, even though it is precisely those comments which throw light on the question of 'nation-state revision *v*. hegemonic great-power politics'.

They are as clear and unambiguous as his warnings about warlike adventures at that point in time. His notes of 12 November 1937[37] are significant in this connection. They disclose his attitude

to Hitler's observations of 5 November 1937, which have been
handed down to us in the Hossbach memorandum. Hence they are
also of particular value as sources and evidence because, being
personal comments, they are largely free of tactical considerations.
Beck wrote, 'I do not dispute the expediency of settling the
Czechoslovakian business (possibly the Austrian one too) when the
opportunity arises and thus of keeping this in mind and of making
preparations within the scope of what is possible.' He formulated
his views more clearly in a note of 29 May 1938 which was
submitted to the army commander-in-chief. In it he refutes point by
point Hitler's speech of the previous day to leading representatives
of the state, the party and the armed forces. First of all, however, he
outlines supposed or actual points of agreement. '(1) It is correct
that Germany needs greater *Lebensraum*, both in Europe and in the
form of colonies. The first can be acquired only by war . . . (2) It is
correct that Czechoslovakia in the form imposed on her by the
Treaty of Versailles is unacceptable to Germany and a way must be
found of eliminating her as a source of danger, by warlike means if
necessary. But in the latter case the outcome must be worth the
while . . .' He even says in a fifth point that it is true that 'there
were various reasons in favour of an early solution by force'. In this
respect he alludes to the continuing rearmament of Great Britain
and France, and to the possibility of favourable realignments as a
result of tension between Italy and the Western powers. He also
notes, however, that 'all these factors' would 'work to our disad-
vantage' as long as Czechoslovakia could count on the armed
assistance of France and England. In what followed he pulled to
pieces one by one Hitler's arguments in favour of 'an early solution
by force' of the Czechoslovakian question.[38]

His memorandum of 3 June 1938, however, shows that he
rejected forcible action solely on the ground that the time was not
ripe: such a conflict, in view of the existing power structure in
Europe, could not be isolated, especially in the face of Czechoslovakia's network of alliances. An adventure of that nature could
not, therefore, be brought to a successful conclusion given the still
inadequate state of the economy and of German rearmament. It
also shows that Beck had no objection *in principle* to Czechoslovakia being rubbed off the political map of Europe. Commenting
on the appendix to the 'Directive for the uniform Preparation of the
Armed Forces for War', he pointed out in his memorandum, 'The

question of overthrowing Czechoslovakia had been continuously examined and worked on since the Reich Defence Minister's order of 4 April 1935 ... and before that by the General Staff of the army. The military necessity of the project had long been recognised within the General Staff at least as clearly as it had been recognised by the authorities competent to decide this question.' In saying this he is referring to the corresponding 'investigations and preliminary studies' carried out 'over many years' by the general staff.[39]

These statements suggest considerably more than a simple 'revision of Versailles, expanded by a claim to the German-speaking areas of the crumbling Danube monarchy'.[40] Are they not also expressive of German claims to a hegemonic role in Central and eastern Central Europe? Expansionist ambitions reveal themselves here which must be taken all the more seriously precisely because they were expressed in connection with warnings against launching a campaign at an inappropriate time. They do not, however, sit easily within a framework of ideas about a modest adjustment of national boundaries. They promise to go well beyond it, at least in the direction of achieving hegemony in Europe. In this regard Beck's notes and memoranda of 1937–38 reveal that his political ideas lay within a tradition descended from the imperialist notions of the Wilhelmine era, which maintained its continuity, even if not unchanged, beyond the collapse of the Kaiser's Reich, and of which the general staff had always been custodian.[41] Beck's struggle to avoid war in 1938 was thus more than 'an attempt to rescue German revisionist policy'; rather, it was an effort to prevent the foundations and prospects of future hegemony in Central Europe from being heedlessly set at risk by Hitler's rash adventure.

Was all this perhaps just a new version of Wilhelmine imperialist policy? To answer in the affirmative would be to misunderstand Beck's views as too static and unrefined; above all, it would be to overlook the development of his thinking. Initially he was concerned not with a purely schematic expansion of the Reich's territory to incorporate the limits of German settlement in Central Europe. He wrote,[42] 'Germany has beyond all doubt a problem of space.' He went on to say that there was still a chance of small territorial adjustments in Europe under certain circumstances, but by and large 'the position of the population of Europe as such had been stable for 1,000 years or more ... so that widespread changes scarcely seemed achievable any more without very serious disruption'. Beck had, thus, a lively sense of the way the disposition of Europe had been determined historically and of the resultant responsibilities.

His notion was more that of an extension of German power in Central Europe by virtue of a position of influence and supremacy, not of annexations that went beyond the union with areas of German-speaking population. He drew a clear distinction between an increase in space and an increase in power. An abyss separated him from Hitler's ideas of 'space'. Nor in Beck is there any trace of Social-Darwinist ideas. On the contrary, he expressly emphasised respect for the right of other nations to exist. Certainly in 1938 he seems to have seen the dominant powers in terms of a scale of importance in European politics with regard to the justification of their actions and their special rights. In the comment on Hitler's speech in the Reich Chancellery of 5 November 1937 which has already been mentioned he reckons with opposition to German ambitions from the other two great European powers, England and France. He continued, 'Politics is the art of the possible; all three nations are on the earth at the same time, and all are in Europe, to boot. That surely means that all possibilities of coming to terms with each other must first be exhausted, especially in view of the relative strength of each. Besides, this is wiser in the event of a later break.' From this and from other observations which have survived it is clear that he did not consider any expansion of German power feasible without the consent of the great powers named. But it follows logically that with their agreement, or rather in the absence of a veto, such an expansion of space and power must definitely be possible. Consequently the countries affected would have to bow to the will of the three great powers. The status for which he strove, that of a position for Germany as a great power, therefore included by definition the disposability of smaller states and nations, in particular those states which had emerged after 1918. His use of the word 'intolerable' in connection with Czechoslovakia supports this view. And the constraint that it was 'first' necessary to try and come to terms with the other great powers, as well as the reference to the possibility of a later rupture in relations with any who stood in the way of German expansion, point unmistakably to the fact that Beck did not exclude military conflict, or at least the application of military pressure, in the event of great-power opposition.

Moreover the passage quoted from Beck's comment on 12 December 1937, and, if anything clearer still, his note of 29 May 1938 show that his opposition to war was not based on principle. In keeping with the spirit of his age he never excluded the use of armed force in resolving disputes between sovereign states.

In conclusion we can state with some confidence that in Beck's mind the idea of Germany as a great power was closely bound up with a feeling of European responsibility and solidarity. At the same time, however, it should be observed that his views on foreign policy were very largely rooted in the Wilhelmine concepts of great-power status and hegemony, even though — and this is very important — those ideas had been considerably modified. Within the bounds of the juxtaposition mentioned — of notions of great-power status *and* of a European consciousness — Beck wanted not only to see the Treaty of Versailles revised, but also to see the Central European scene fundamentally transformed in terms of Germany supremacy. After the Anschluss with Austria and the elimination of Czechoslovakia from power politics the strength of German supremacy would naturally extend far into Central and South-eastern Europe.

Methodologically, this concept of hegemony was to be realised by a combination of growing military strength and political alliances. This did not necessarily and inevitably imply war, but nor did it in essence exclude it, either. Beck was never an opponent of war on principle. His scheme did envisage 'sensible', i.e. limited, armed conflicts, to be kept under control politically — but not a 'great' war and not necessarily war at all.

Beck's military and rearmament policies fit into the framework of such calculation. Germany must become so strong militarily that , in the situations of conflict which would inevitably arise in trying to realise her ambitions, the Reich's armed might was such as either to keep other great powers at a distance from the outset or to finish the necessary military engagements off so speedily and completely that no intervention by third parties could be swift enough to succeed; or even so that the intended aim could be achieved by a show of force alone. Intermittent attempts at compromise and military alliances could also serve the same purpose. In this vein Beck pointed out in criticising Hitler's statements of 5 November 1937 that, as there were 'various grounds for an early solution by force' of the Czechoslovak question, it was necessary to clarify 'political approaches with the powers which were on our side or which were not against us'. Even 'military discussions' were to be entered into 'in some cases'. Moreover he was even critical of the evident neglect of military negotiations, which should have been conducted with Hungary, for instance, in preparing for an intervention against Czechoslovakia.

Here Beck was alluding to proceedings which went back to 1935 and to which he had since devoted particular attention.[43] At that time, on the occasion of the visit of the Hungarian chief of staff, he had discussed with the Secretary of State in the Foreign Office, von Bülow, the possibility of a joint German-Hungarian venture against Czechoslovakia and had taken pains to further the realisation of this plan. In pursuing this course he was able to continue talks which Goering had begun during a visit to Budapest in May 1935. On that occasion the second most important figure in Hitler's state had also broached the subject of joint action against Czechoslovakia. Bülow and Beck were agreed that a solution of the Czechoslovak problem would be difficult. It is apparent from the record of the talks that both, however, were of the opinion that the answer could only lie in power politics and a decisive act of aggression, with the aim of 'partitioning Czechoslovakia'. A prerequisite would be the 'agreement of the aggressors involved and . . . the indifference or containment of third parties'.

Henceforth Beck intensified his contacts with the Hungarian army in pursuance of such political and military considerations. He himself went to Budapest in September 1935. He was evidently able to lay the foundations of a sort of secret military diplomacy, which was to create the conditions for subsequent joint action against Czechoslovakia. Again in September 1937 he held direct talks with the Hungarian Defence Minister and temporary chief of the general staff, Racz, in this connection, without informing his Minister and highest military superior, Field Marshal von Blomberg. According to statements made by the Hungarian Defence Minister, Beck is supposed to have been preparing military plans with the Hungarians for a move against Czechoslovakia in 1940.[44]

If this policy of military alliance was one component in the process of realising the conception of great power politics as represented by Beck, then rearmament policy formed the other component.[45] Contrary to the interpretation which has prevailed up to now in the literature, the Chief of the General Staff urged on with all his energy the re-equipment of the army on a massive scale from the outset. In this he was in complete agreement with the supreme command of the armed forces. When he assumed his duties as Chief of the General Staff, (Troop Office) in October 1933 the fundamental decision on the nature of German rearmament had already been taken. The Reich withdrew from the Disarmament Conference and the League of Nations. From now on Germany would rearm autonomously and unilaterally, regardless of international agreements, obligations or consultation. This course corresponded completely with Beck's own views. Moreover he was not at all pleased when Hitler initially informed foreign countries of a lower rate of rearmament than that provided for in the armed forces' plans. Like Blomberg, Beck had always been an adherent of autonomous rearmament free of the constraints of collective systems and multipartite treaties. He was likewise an uncompromising devotee of an army of universal conscription, organised and led by the traditional military leadership caste. A 'League of Nations army', a militia, even a politicised people's militia, had no place in his thinking. At the end of 1933, therefore, there was no divergence of opinion, conceptually or politically, between the Minister and the new Chief of the Troop Office. And at that time both men had Hitler's full trust.

There was naturally an element of risk in deciding on unilateral rearmament which was not safeguarded multilaterally by a system of international agreements. Hitler and Blomberg both realised this, and it soon caused Beck some concern, but like the political leadership he consciously accepted it. Such rearmament and military policies which already bore elements of risk were at bottom the consequence of a train of thought which intended to make Germany a great power and which envisaged the Reich only in terms of a Germany 'large, strong . . . and independent'. The independent and therefore risky rearmament policy corresponded fully with the rationale of this view of great-power status.

Beck recognised the threshold of risk, of course. Hence his support for speedy and full-scale rearmament from the outset in order to bring the phase of risk to an end as quickly as possible. Of related concern was his call for the introduction of universal conscription earlier than the date scheduled for it by Hitler and the Minister of the Armed Forces, summer 1934, then autumn 1934, but at first he was unable to make his voice heard. At the end of

1933 he wanted to know that an army of thirty-one divisions instead of twenty-one had been fixed as the planned target. He pressed for the abolition of the demilitarised zone of the Rhineland at the end of 1934, for, as command exercises ('war games') had shown, the rearmament plans of December 1933 could not be realised in terms of either personnel or materials without the region's resources.[46]

Beck's dynamism and readiness to modify established standards and views of the military structure are revealed in the extraordinary decisions in the area of personnel planning by means of which he was willing to hurry along the rebuilding and enlargement of the army for reasons of policy and strategy. When the Chief of the Army Personnel Office protested against over-hasty rearmament because of worries about the declining proportion of officers in the army, Beck asserted his will on the side of no slackening of the pace. In his plans of 1933 he had estimated the ratio of officers at 7%. During the build-up period it could be allowed to fall to 4%. But by 1936 the percentage of officers had fallen to 1·6. Yet Beck carried through unchecked his build-up against the doubts of the Army Personnel Office. He countered its warnings of a fall in the quantity and quality of the officer corps in its old sense by enlisting officers from the paramilitary Land police, the Landespolizei, and by promoting more noncommissioned officers. The needs of the time, compel such measures, the General Staff argued.[47]

Beck was driven by anxiety to get through the danger period as quickly as possible — the period when the arbiters of Versailles could still take sanctions before Germany was in a position to defy them. In the meantime Beck's original calculation had been proved wrong. The Reich found itself in a precarious position. Unilateral, forced rearmament had in no sense improved Germany's position in terms of political security. Rather, a disastrous arms race seemed to loom on the horizon. France decided to modernise its army, as also to set about creating a counterbalance to the Reich's growing might by including the Soviet Union in its plans and by consolidating its systems of alliances. All in all, the European situation had been destabilised, not least by unilateral German rearmament unfettered by treaty.

Beck recognised this perfectly well. He responded to the destabilisation of the European scene, first, with the demand that the Reich's foreign policy must at all costs avoid any provocation of other powers. He would not and could not, however, dispose of the root cause of the problem, the one thing that other countries saw as the greatest provocation; German rearmament. It was impossible for him in the light of the premises and principles of his political thought. Thus at the end of 1934 he noted approvingly the analysis of the situation by his closest adviser on military policy, which stated , 'If one examines the present possibilities of strengthening Germany's military-political situation they include the attempt to dispel England's apprehensions, in particular about the arming of the Luftwaffe.' But a note immediately followed: 'Any renunciation of further rearmament in the air is naturally out of the question.'[48] If therefore Beck was demanding that German diplomacy should shield German rearmament in the international arena, and defuse its provocative character, then, under the circumstances, he was asking the Wilhelmstrasse to square the circle.

Beck's second response to the destabilisation of the situation in Europe was a further acceleration and intensification of rearmament. In an analysis of the situation in July 1935 he acknowledged an 'instability in political relations within Europe' and called for 'completion' of the programme of rearmament which was to be 'interrupted as little as possible and limited to the shortest possible time'.[49] Towards the end of the year he began to plan and then to put together a large, motorised 'assault army' consisting of motorised, mechanised and heavily armoured units. A memorandum of the general staff's Organisation Department stated that the previously 'planned number of tank units would be a long way short of what was needed to enable the army to take the offensive in the event of war', hence the requirement to 'build up an army capable of carrying out a decisive war of aggression'.[50] In a memorandum of December 1935[51] Beck therefore provided for a considerably larger number of tank units and motorised troops than previously, which would ultimately form almost a third of the army's large units. In this context the Chief of the General Staff repeatedly made it clear that financial considerations should not be allowed to stand in the way. In the submissions of the Organisation Department he deleted all suggestions for effecting economies which would have tended to impair the basic model of the planned army as outlined. In another memorandum of 30 January 1936 with which he answered objections from the AHA he asserted unequivocally, 'In view of the increasingly accepted recognition of the importance of the tank weapon for the strike capability of modern armies .. I would not consider it wise to make cuts from the outset in the number of forty-eight tank battalions which are deemed necessary on the basis of our military and political situation *out of financial considerations.'.*[52]

One hears it said again and again that Beck, unlike Guderian, the pioneer of the operational tank force, had no appreciation of its importance.[53] Put in those terms, the statement is incorrect. Beck called for and planned more tank units than Guderian was asking for at the time.[54] Yet Guderian's version, claiming that Beck was an opponent of such a tank force, initially prevailed after the war, even though it was not in accordance with the historical evidence. In contrast to Guderian's version, however, Beck was in fact positively well disposed towards the organisation of tank units into divisions. Until enough experience of commanding such units had been gained, however, he wanted to raise as many tank battalions as possible, mostly massed in brigades, but only three tank divisions as experimental units. He organised the creation of tank units and motorised units in such a way that they could be speedily combined to form tank divisions in the event of this form of organisation proving itself. He supported the operational use of tank divisions in principle. He was not at all in favour of the French doctrine of tank warfare but he was strong in his emphasis that only the use of tank divisions could bring success in the case of operationally 'long-range targets'.[55]

In the last analysis Beck's vision of December 1935 amounted to a fundamental restructuring of previous rearmament planning. When the build-up of the army was complete, over a third of the operational strength was intended to consist of motorised and tank units. The following example shows with what energy Beck hastened the build-up of such a force in view of the 'instability of political relations in Europe'. At the beginning of 1934 the Chief of the General Staff was still agreeing with the head of the Ordnance Department when the latter referred emphatically in a lecture to the need during the course of the planned rearmament not to lose sight of the realities of finance and production.[56] But over two years later the general situation in Europe had changed to a great extent — not least on account of German rearmament — and Beck was no longer able to adhere to these principles. In August 1936 the AHA pointed out to him and to the commander-in-chief of the army that after

Beck's plans for assembling an army capable of long-range offensive operations had been carried out, the armament industry would
suffer from considerable overcapacity. The danger would then arise
of a demobilisation crisis with all its imponderable political, social
and economic consequences, unless the army were put to use.[57] The
alternative would be to change the programme and timing of the
rearmament. Beck and the commander-in-chief rejected any change
in the programme. Indeed, on 6 December 1936[58] Fritsch ordered
its continuation. The build-up was supposed to be completed in the
period between 1940 and 1943. Thus the alternatives — to rearm
at immense cost or to accept a demobilisation crisis, or even to
consider deploying the army in the field, were not forced on the
army command by Hitler. It was a consequence of the planning
which had been conceived by Beck and ordered by Fritsch. At the
end of 1936, therefore, Beck was faced with a fearful dilemma, and
apparently all he could do was consciously put up with it. The
general staff's rearmament plans had overstepped the borderline
between defensive and offensive rearmament. Developments had
thus received an impetus which was soon to get out of control.

V

A path had been taken which was ultimately to lead the Chief of the
General Staff into a hopeless situation. So much was apparent
from the end of 1937. In the famous conference of 5 November
1937 in the Reich Chancellery Hitler justified the warlike expansionist policy he was pursuing not only on the grounds of raw
material and foreign exchange problems but above all in terms of
the pressure of time due to the arms race. On that occasion he
argued that Germany would be militarily superior to its potential
enemies only for a short period of time. It was imperative to exploit
that period. That the Führer could argue in this way was the result
not least of the rearmament policy conceived largely by Beck. For
all the scheduled dates of the army's expansion pointed without
question in the direction indicated by Hitler. In addition, the
operational plans and exercises of the general staff had since 1935
to an increasing extent dealt with the question of a speedy military
overthrow of Czechoslovakia.[59]
    In the first instance the strategic aim of such an action was to
provide the Reich with the security in its rear which was necessary

for a successful defence against France within the framework of a Central European war on several fronts. From the end of 1938 a possible posture of events loomed in which a future position of military strength might allow of direct action against Czechoslovakia in order to improve the Reich's strategic position by a quantum leap, given a favourable situation throughout Europe. Beck did indeed criticise the detail of Hitler's comments of 5 November 1937 but with regard to Czechoslovakia he was essentially in agreement, even if he did not indicate in specific terms the point in time or the preconditions. His medium-term view with regard to the elimination of Czechoslovakia from the political scene evidently concurred in principle with Hitler's views. The agreed building of the West Wall together with the results of the massive rearmament would soon make such a course possible just as the necessities of finance and production already mentioned would make it imperative. Beck had been making his preparations for these eventualities since November 1937. He exerted a decisive influence on the armed forces' directives of 7 and 12 December 1937,[60] which, although they assumed that there would not be a war against Czechoslovakia in 1938, did designate the adjustment and intensification of operational planning for such an operation 'Green' as urgent. Similarly in December he ordered the completion of corresponding large-scale exercises by the general staff and considered further agreements on military policy and strategy with Hungary.[61] For Beck, who was convinced of the necessity of solving 'the Czech problem' at a suitable date, these exercises were an indispensable but not an urgent part of the preparations. They were commensurate with the overall situation and in accordance with directives. And in these directives it was *Beck's* views, not those of Hitler — which in Beck's eyes had not been fully worked out — that had found expression. The annual 'street ride' (a war game in which the highest-ranking general staff officers and generals normally took part) could therefore be undertaken in the belief that it did not imply an immediate realisation of Hitler's aims as they had been revealed on 5 November. But what if in spite of its plausibility this belief proved unfounded? That the army was still not ready was incontestable. What *was* open to question, in view of the ambivalent unfolding of the international situation, was when the right moment for the switch to a policy of pressure and expansion backed by military support could be said to have arrived.

In this regard a dictatorial state leadership could very speedily destroy such innocence.

Looking back with hindsight on the outcome of the events of spring and summer 1938, the observer discerns with frightening clarity the dilemma faced by the advocates of a military revisionist policy in a dictatorship where the authoritarian Führer understood how to eliminate the military command as a political factor, and how to reduce it to a merely functional elite, as happened just at that time with the removal of its senior representatives in the Fritsch—Blomberg crisis.

In a situation where the military leadership was no longer an independent authority, even if it still saw itself as such, any professional military measure such as the general staff exercise mentioned above, any operational blueprint, or any decision of military policy such as, for instance, to build up a motorised and mechanised army of the offensive, was open to manipulation. Moreover any of these could, in an extreme case, work against the intentions of the military command responsible. On the one hand, an exercise such as the planned manoeuvres was, in the light of developments in both rearmament and politics, both technically and chronologically appropriate. On the other, since a negative outcome was not excluded from the beginning, it might tend dangerously to support the decisions of the political leadership. In the eyes of the Chief of the General Staff these were unwelcome because they were fraught with risk but which, after Hitler had spoken his mind on 5 November 1937, did not lie beyond the bounds of possibility. This would bring the senior military officers, headed by the commander-in-chief of the army and the Chief of the General Staff, into a position where the outcome of their activities, particularly in view of the current potential of the military machine, would reinforce the political decisions of the nation's leaders without leaving them any scope to steer events in a direction of their choosing.

In 1938, therefore, Beck faced a public crisis in the rearmament policy of which he was the originator. The overriding hopelessness of the army command's military policy became clear at the very moment when the dictator was beginning to launch the policy of aggression for which, in Beck's opinion, the time was not ripe nor the military machine ready. The conflict which broke out between him and Hitler in the circumstances, and which finally ended in his resignation, has often been described and analysed.[62] Initially such accounts were offered in the name of his 'struggle to avert war', a struggle which, even if it was in vain and conducted with inappropriate means, would always ensure him an honourable place in history. Furthermore, prominence was given as the central factor in this conflict to his attempts to create a suitable structure of power that would include top representatives of both the military and the civil authority. Such analyses reflect a crucial aspect in his way of thinking, namely the claim on behalf of the military leadership to a share in decision-making and responsibility at the highest political level, beyond the bounds of a department of state. But the conflict had a third dimension which in the last analysis points to the dilemma of German military policy and of the aspiration to great-power status.

From May 1938 it had become increasingly clear to Beck, on the strength of Hitler's order at the end of April to make concrete preparations for a conflict with Czechoslovakia, that the Führer intended belligerent action that same year. He admitted to a confidant[63] in November that he had had only one thought since May: 'How can I prevent a war?' He was deeply convinced that a war against Germany's neighbour to the south-east could not be contained and that the Reich was still in no position to conduct a European war with any hope of success, especially as Great Britain's entry would immediately lend it global dimensions.

His attempts to avert an onslaught which would be catastrophic for the German nation-state developed methodically in two stages. In the first phase the Chief of the General Staff tried to reach his goal by way of normal, official channels. He submitted memoranda to his commander-in-chief and lectured him in the hope of inducing him to intervene decisively with the head of state. His essential arguments were concerned with politics, military policy and rearmament.[64] In the second phase Beck sought his objective – the avoidance of war – by taking extraordinary steps, such as, for instance, suggesting to his commander-in-chief that the most senior generals should resign *en bloc* in the eventuality of Hitler adhering to his policy of war. Ultimately he even contemplated pressure verging on rebellion, in the shape of military action against the 'radical forces' which he saw at work behind Hitler's war plans, coupled with the threat of resignation by all the generals. The political shock which would probably result from collective resignation was intended to be the occasion for an 'internal clean sweep'.[65] Such consolidation was not meant primarily to obviate politico-moral blemishes on the face of the regime, but rather to eliminate the 'radical elements' which Beck held responsible for the international game of chance. These were precisely the forces which had continued to jeopardise the position of the army command and the officer corps in domestic politics since 1933–34. Now, when it was a matter of 'war or peace', Beck saw them and their irresponsible intrigues at work again. In his procedural suggestions, therefore, the struggle against a disastrous war policy joined the long-standing conflict about the army's position, role and influence in the state.

In this regard the domestic dimension of his suggestions at the time referred back to his activities in the Röhm affair and to his contacts with Ludendorff some years before. Alluding urgently to the fact that it was no longer merely a question of war and peace but that it was also a matter of the army's power base in the state, Beck tried to rouse the commander-in-chief and the leading generals to action in a final desperate attempt. He pointed out to the commander-in-chief that Hitler seemed totally under the influence of these 'radical circles'. He reported that the Führer was supposed to have explained to a small circle, 'I have to conduct the war against Czechoslovakia with the old generals. I shall conduct the war against England and France with a new body of leaders'.[66] Could the Chief of the General Staff have referred more bluntly to the direct danger of the failure of the traditional concept of participation in power? It was now a question of opposing at the eleventh hour the danger of a disastrous politics of war. And the danger had been able to arise at least partly because the share in decision-making which Beck had demanded had been contested.

However, the commander-in-chief of the army and the leading generals did not follow the Chief of the General Staff's compelling projections. Beck resigned from his post, in protest against Hitler's war policy, but also because he had been unable to persuade his commander-in-chief and his fellow generals to his point of view. He wrote bitterly to a former colleague that the conditions of his remaining in office no longer applied. And, later still, looking back in anger, he remarked several times that in the final analysis he had been left in the lurch.[67] Subsequent writers have very largely accepted his own verdict on the supreme army command and have severly censured the generals concerned, the commander-in chief, von Brauchitsch, first among them, for not following his suggestions or his example. In view of the fatal consequences of Hitler's policies, which culminated in the destruction of Bismarck's nation-state, the criticism is cetainly justified in historical terms. But a detailed analysis makes it clear that the actual situation was more complicated than can be conveyed in a study which seeks only to attribute individual responsibility with hindsight. It also makes it clear that at the same time Beck's failure reveals the depth of despair to which the army command's military and rearmament policies had led the Chief of the General Staff. The development of Hitler's ideas on politics and the military as they had become discernible from 5 November 1937 at the latest had already made evident the political quandary into which the army command, because of its rearmament policy, had fallen *vis-à-vis* the dictator. Beck's unsuccessful attempt to galvanise his commander-in-chief and his fellow generals into action revealed his failure at the professional level as well. Since the existing rearmament and military policies did not allow of any other real alternative he had, as things stood, to convince his immediate superior and the leading generals that a war against Czechoslovakia could not be contained and, in view of the French intervention which he regarded as certain, to say nothing of the British, could not be won. But in the summer of 1938 he failed to make any impression. There were at least three reasons.

Firstly, the reports of the German military attachés in the most important European capitals, above all in Paris and in London, did not reveal with total clarity between May and August 1938 that the Western powers would necessarily commit themselves militarily in a German conflict with Czechoslovakia.[68] It was reported from Paris, for instance, among other things, that the French would not intervene if the Germans proceeded to react as in self-defence on the Sudeten Germans' behalf in the face of Czech intransigence or acts of provocation. As Secretary of State Weizsäcker noted at that time, even he saw room for Germany to manoeuvre in the case of provocative acts by the Czechs. And at the beginning of May 1938 the German military attaché in London had reported that, despite advanced discussions between the French and British general staffs, he was 'firmly convinced that there were still many loopholes open for a peaceful and evolutionary settlement of additional and legitimate German interests'.

Secondly, in May 1938 the general staff's intelligence sub-department Foreign Armies West had also disclosed in a comprehensive study of possible French operational intentions that, in the event of war, French attacks would not have to be reckoned with at once but, if at all, perhaps from the fifth day on at the earliest. The German military attaché in Paris, too, had declared an immediate offensive improbable. Moreover in summer 1937 the Department of Foreign Armies West had submitted a detailed analysis of the attitude of the French leadership which ended in the prognosis that a French first offensive was highly improbable; rather, the idea of the *retour offensif* corresponded more to the thinking of the French leadership. In contrast with the view of the Chief of the General Staff, scepticism about the possibility of an immediate offensive by the French army on the outbreak of war was evidently widespread in the relevant department of the general staff, and seemed well founded.[69]

Thirdly, Beck had stated in his memoranda that at least three weeks would be needed to overthrow Czeckoslovakia. The western front, therefore, would have to withstand a French offensive alone for longer than fourteen days. But on 16 June 1938 the results were available of the large-scale general staff exercise, which, in keeping with Beck's orders, was supposed to simulate a campaign against Czechoslovakia with the simultaneous entry into the war of the Western powers and to examine the probable course of events. They provided no conclusive evidence to support Beck's views. Rather, the opposite was the case. The Czech forces had been disposed of in only eleven days. The motorised and tank units were withdrawn from the front and placed as a reserve force at the disposal of the army command. The transfer of the first two divisions to the western front had been possible after only seven days. Four more days later, two army corps with three divisions could be moved to the west.[70]

This meant that, from a professional military point of view, Beck had no convincing and conclusive arguments or evidence to back the soundness of his appraisal of the situation. Neither the reports of the military attachés nor the study by the army's Intelligence nor the result of the war games supported his view.

It was therefore not altogether surprising that the commander-in-chief of the army and the majority of the senior generals had reservations about agreeing to his extraordinary plans for action against Hitler's policy of war. For them the situation, seen from a purely military standpoint, was not at all clear-cut. Beck's resignation was in this respect more a sign of submission to fate than a symbol of rebellion. There he stood, empty-handed. He could not demonstrate the certain operational fiasco of a campaign against Czechoslovakia; on the contrary, there was much to refute it, not least the result of the general staff exercise. Likewise the prognosis that Britain and France would be sure to intervene remained by its very nature a matter of opinion. As Weizsäcker, too, emphasised, it all boiled down to the prospects for a German offensive. The commander-in-chief and the senior generals were agreed that a world war meant the end of Germany, but they were not convinced beyond all doubt that such a war would necessarily result from the Czech conflict. They were, however, certain that the armed forces were strong enough to tackle Czechoslovakia. None of this alters the fact that Beck's long-term view was right. For he thought within the framework of world politics while the other generals thought in purely military terms and in categories limited to Central Europe. But the situation in 1938 was not precisely as clear-cut on the military level as it may seem in restrospect.

Within a larger framework his failure was symptomatic of the dilemma of the great-power politics backed by the military. The Chief of the General Staff had been led into the dilemma by a military and rearmament policy at the heart of which lay expansionist aims. For him the ends were based on traditional views of hegemony, but in Hitler's conception they had taken on altogether wider dimensions. This military and rearmament policy had contributed substantially to the fact that the greatest powers of Europe, even those which had been open to a revision of Versailles by agreement, were ultimately compelled to take counter-measures. Equally they contributed to the fact that as soon as it was ready Hitler was tempted to make use of the instrument of military power which had been built. This, in Beck's view, was at an irresponsibly early stage. But, in view of the reactions which rearmament had evoked, and in view of its economically intolerable scale, was there in fact a 'right' time? Given the objectives of the national-conservative ruling elite, there was no way out of the dilemma posed by the costs of rearmament, which in the long run were economically and socially intolerable, and the reactions of the great powers.

Some months later Ludwig Beck said to a confidant, 'I warned them – and in the end I was alone!'[71] His commander-in-chief and the leading generals had not followed him in his 'struggle to avert war'; but the dilemma of his rearmament policy and with it the hopeless contradictions of great-power politics, backed by the military, had caught up with him.

Notes

1 The following remarks summarise some of the essential findings of a thorough examination and documentation which the author has published under the title *General Ludwig Beck. Studien und Dokumente zur politisch-militärischen Vorstellungswelt und Tätigkeit des Generalstabschefs des deutschen Heeres 1933–1938*, Boppard, 1980 (Schriftenreihe des Bundesarchivs). It contains comprehensive references to source materials and analyses of the literature. Footnotes here are therefore kept to a minimum. The book has caused a controversial debate: Peter Hoffmann, 'Generaloberst Becks militär-politisches Denken', *Historische Zeitschrift*, 234, 1982, pp. 101–21, and Klaus-Jürgen Müller, 'Militärpolitik, nicht Militäropposition! Eine Erwiderung', *Historische Zeitschrift*, 235, 1982, pp. 355–371; cf. also the discussion in Jürgen Schmädeke and Peter Steinbach, *Der Widerstand gegen den Nationalsozialismus. Die deutsche Gesellschaft und der Widerstand gegen Hitler*, Munich and Zürich, 1985, pp. 1119–58.

2 Ulrich von Hassell, *Vom anderen Deutschland. Aus den nachgelassenen Tagebüchern 1938–1940*, Frankfurt a. M., 1964 (Fischer-Bücherei 605), p. 228, entry of 24 March 1942.

3 Wolfgang Foerster, *Generaloberst Ludwig Beck. Sein Kampf gegen den Krieg. Aus den nachgelassenen Papieren des Generalstabschefs*, Munich, 1953 (new edition: *Ein General kämpft gegen den Krieg*, Munich, 1949); Gert Buchheit, *Ludwig Beck. Ein preussischer General*, Munich, 1964; and Nicholas Reynolds, *Treason was no Crime: Ludwig Beck, Chief of General Staff*, London, 1976. See the author's review of this book in *Militärgeschichtliche Mitteilungen*, XXV, 1979, pp. 228–30.

4 On this problem see the next chapter in the present volume.

5 Cf. K.-J. Müller, 'Probleme seiner Biographie', *Militärgeschichtliche Mitteilungen*, XI, 1972, p. 167 ff. The thoughtful study by Peter Hoffmann, *Widerstand gegen Hitler. Probleme des Umsturzes*, Munich, 1979, again reflects these two tendencies. In his examination, which is of a consciously political and ethical nature and places emphasis on personalities, he fundamentally misjudges both the methodical approach intended by me (p. 11) and the content of my position in the case of General Beck (p. 12) as well as its critical detachment from Reynolds's interpretations of Beck. See *Militärges-*

chichtliche Mitteilungen, XXV, 1979, pp. 228–30.

6   On the following see K.-J. Müller, *General Beck*, chapter IV, and Wilhelm Deist, 'Das militärische Instrument für den Krieg', chapter II in Militärgeschichtliches Forschungsamt (ed.), *Das Deutsche Reich und der Zweite Weltkrieg*, vol. 1, *Ursachen und Voraussetzungen der deutschen Kriegspolitik*, Stuttgart, 1979, and *id.*, *The Wehrmacht and German Rearmament*, London, 1981, and Michael Geyer, *Aufrüstung oder Sicherheit. Die Reichswehr und die Krise der Machtpolitik*, Wiesbaden, 1980.

7   K.-J. Müller, 'Reichswehr und "Röhm-Affäre"'. Aus den Akten des Wehrkreiskommandos (Bayer.) VII', *Militärgeschichtliche Mitteilungen*, III 1968, pp. 107–44, and *id.*, *General Beck*, chapters II and IV.

8   Printed as document 11 in K.-J. Müller, *General Beck*.

9   Cf. Hans Speidel, 'Ludwig Beck', in *Die grossen Deutschen*, I, Berlin, 1956, and *id.*, *Zeitbetrachtungen*, Stuttgart, 1969, and *id.*, *Aus unserer Zeit, Erinnerungen*, Frankfurt a. M., Berlin and Vienna, 1977, and Foerster, *Beck* p. 64 ff.

10   Wilhelm Ritter von Schramm, *Beck und Goerdeler. Gemeinschaftsdokumente für den Frieden 1941 bis 1944*, Munich, 1965, pp. 26, 30, 45.

11   Cf. K.-J. Müller, *Das Heer und Hitler. Armee und nationalsozialistisches Regime 1933–1940*, Stuttgart, 1969, p. 234 ff, and documents Nos. 29 and 30, therein (exchange of letters between Beck and Kühlenthal, from which the following quotations also come. Emphases by the author).

12   Cf. Speidel, *Aus unserer Zeit*, especially p. 349 ff. See also the explanations of the retired Panzer general, Leo Freiherr Geyr von Schweppenburg, in Archiv des Militärgeschichtlichen Forschungsamtes, Freiburg i. Br.

13   The following quotations come from documents Nos. 1 and 45 in K.-J. Müller, *General Beck*, and the document cited in Foerster, *Beck*, p. 60.

14   Cf. The memorandum 'The Objective' printed in W. Ritter von Schramm, *Beck und Goerdeler*, and see in general Hermann Graml, 'Die aussenpolitischen Vorstellungen des deutschen Widerstandes', in Walter Schmitthenner and Hans Buchheim (eds.), *Der deutsche Widerstand gegen Hitler. Vier historisch-kritische Studien*, Cologne and Berlin, 1966.

15   Cf. K.-J. Müller, *General Beck*, chapters IV and V.

16   In addition to the publication cited in the previous note see also for the following K.-J. Müller, 'Staat und Politik im Denken Ludwig Becks', *Historische Zeitschrift*, CCXV, 1972, pp. 608–31.

17   Ludwig Beck, *Studien*, ed. Hans Speidel, Stuttgart, 1955, for the studies from which the following quotations come.

18   On this point and the following see K.-J. Müller, 'Staat und Politik im Denken Ludwig Becks', p. 617 ff, and the relevant references printed there.

19   Beck, *Studien*, p. 35 ff.

20   Cf. the comments in Manfred Messerschmidt, *Militär und Politik in der Bismarckzeit und im wilhelmmischen Deutschland*, Darmstadt, 1975 (Erträge der Forschung), and Andreas Hillgruber, 'Kontinuität und Diskontinuität in der Aussenpolitik von Bismarck bis Hitler', in *id.*, *Grossmachtpolitik und der Militarismus im zwanzigsten Jahrhundert. Drei Beiträge zum Kontinuitätsproblem*, Düsseldorf, 1964. There are references to further works in these two publications. See, too, the remarks made in the first chapter of the present volume.

21   On this point see Michael Geyer, *Aufrüstung oder Sicherheit. Die Reichswehr und die Krise der Machtpolitik*, Wiesbaden, 1980, and *id.*, 'Die Geschichte des deutschen Militärs von 1860 bis 1945. Ein Bericht über die Forschungslage (1945–1975)', in *Die moderne deutsche Geschichte in der internationalen Forschung 1945–1975*, ed. Hans-Ulrich Wehler (Geschichte und Gesellschaft, No. 4, 1978), pp. 256–58, and *id.*, *Militarismus, Rüstung und Landesverteidigung*.

22   Cf. K.-J. Müller, *General Beck*, chapters I-IV.

23   *Ibid.*, document No. 8.

24   Speech of 30 January 1934: Max Domarus, *Hitler, Reden 1932 bis 1945*, I, p. 355, and the speech of 9 November 1933, *ibid.*, p. 328; in general on the 'twin pillar' theory see K.-J. Müller, *Das Heer und Hitler*, chapter II, especially p. 67 ff, and Manfred Messerschmidt, *Die Wehrmacht im NS-Staat. Zeit der Indokrination*, Hamburg, 1969, chapters I and II, and the summary based on these two works in Michael Salewski, *Wehrmacht und Nationalsozialismus 1933–1939*, Munich, 1978 (Handbuch zur deutschen Militärgeschichte 1648–1939, IV).

25   For details on this point and the following, K.-J. Müller, *Das Heer und Hitler*, chapters V and VI, and *id.*, *General Beck*, chapter III.

26   Quotations in Jodl's diary (IMT XXVIII, p. 374, document PS-1780) and in Keitel's declaration IMT XL, p. 362 ff. On Keitel, too, see *Generalfeldmarschall Keitel. Verbrecher oder Offizier? Erinnerungen, Briefe, Dokumente des Chefs OKW*, ed. Walter Görlitz, Göttingen, Berlin and Frankfurt a. M., 1961, and on Jodl, Luise Jodl, *Jenseits des Endes. Leben und Sterben des Generaloberst Alfred Jodl*, Vienna, Munich, Zurich and Innsbruck, 1976, especially p. 109 ff.

27   Detailed account with references in K.-J. Müller, *General Beck*, chapter II.

28   Thus Foerster, *Beck*, p. 19 ff., and, if with a somewhat different emphasis, N. Reynolds, *Beck. Gehorsam und Widerstand*, pp. 57 ff., 64 ff. (English trans., *Treason was no Crime*, 1976).

29   K.-J. Müller, *General Beck*, document 55.

30   Quotations in Bundesarchiv, Nachlass Holtzmann, No. 31.

31   *Ibid.* See also the literature cited in note 27.

32   In addition to the works by Deist, Geyer and Müller cited in note 6 see also M. Geyer, 'Militär, Rüstung und Aussenpolitik. Aspekte militärischer Revisionspolitik in der Zwischenkriegszeit', in Manfred Funke (ed.), *Hitler, Deutschland und die Mächte. Materialien zur Aussenpolitik des Dritten Reiches*, Düsseldorf, 1976, pp. 239–68,

and Hans-Jürgen Rautenberg, 'Deutsche Rüstungspolitik vom Beginn der Genfer Abrüstungskonferenz bis zur Wiedereinführung der Allgemeinen Wehrpflicht 1932–1935', Ph.D. thesis Bonn, 1971, and *id.*, 'Drei Dokumente zur Planung eines 300,000-Mann-Friedensheeres aus dem Dezember 1933', *Militärgeschichtliche Mitteilungen*, XXII, 1977, pp. 103–39, and M. Geyer, 'Das Zweite Rüstungsprogramm (1930–1934)', *Militärgeschichtliche Mitteilungen*, XVII, 1975, pp. 125–72.

33 On the following see the analysis of Beck's ideas in K.-J. Müller, 'Ludwig Beck – Ein General zwischen Wilhelmismus und Nationalsozialismus', in Imanuel Geiss und Bernd-Jürgen Wendt (eds.), *Deutschland in der Weltpolitik des neunzehnten und zwanzigsten Jahrhunderts*, Düsseldorf, 1973, pp. 513–28.

34 On this point see Hugh Trevor-Roper, 'Hitlers Kriegziele', *Vierteljahrshefte für Zeitgeschichte*, VIII, 1960, p. 126 ff., and the work of H. Graml cited in note 14 above.

35 See G. Niedhart's comprehensive introduction to *Kriegsbeginn 1939. Entfesselung oder Ausbruch des Zweiten Weltkrieges?*, ed. Gottfried Niedhart, Darmstadt, 1976, (Wege der Forschung, 374) and the contributions in parts I and II in the collection by M. Funke (ed.), *Hitler, Deutschland und die Mächte*, Düsseldorf, 1976.

36 On this point see, in addition to the work cited in note 33 above, Reynolds, *Beck*, p. 127 ff.

37 Printed in K.-J. Müller, *General Beck*, document 43.

38 *Ibid.*, document 46.

39 *Ibid.*, document 47.

40 Thus H. Graml, 'Aussenpolitische Vorstellungen', p. 22.

41 On the problem of continuity see A. Hillgruber, 'Kontinuität und Diskontinuität in der deutschen Aussenpolitik von Bismarck bis Hitler', 1974, and with a different emphasis the standard survey in Fritz Fischer, *Bündnis der Eliten. Zur Kontinuität der Machtstrukturen in Deutschland 1871–1945*, Düsseldorf, 1979.

42 K.-J. Müller, *General Beck*, document 46, record of 29 May 1938.

43 Details on this in K.-J. Müller, *General Beck*, chapters IV-VI and documents 31–3.

44 Reynolds, *Beck*, p. 89.

45 On this point and the following see the works cited in notes 6 and 32 above, especially those of Deist.

46 See documents 9, 11, 12 and 17 in K.-J. Müller, *General Beck*.

47 On the size of the officer corps see Rudolf Absolon, *Die Wehrmacht im Dritten Reich*, III (3 August 1934 – 4 February 1938), Boppard, 1975, p. 162. The quotation is in a communication of the general staff's Organisation Department of 24 June 1936 to be found in Bundesarchiv-Militärarchiv, RH 2/v. 1015; the warnings of the Army Personnel Office are in a communication of the same department of 15 June 1935, to be found in Bundesarchiv-Militärarchiv, RH 2/v. 1019.

48 Documents 13 and 14 in K.-J. Müller, *General Beck*.

49 *Ibid.*, document 34.
50 Lecture note of the general staff's Organisation Department of 29
    November 1935 to be found in Bundesarchiv-Militärarchiv, II H
    662; furthermore it was stated in this document: '. . . intentions of
    creating an army capable of a decisive war of aggression by increasing
    its attacking strength and manoeuvrability as the ultimate goal.'
51 Document 37 in K.-J. Müller, *General Beck.*
52 Document 39 in K.-J. Müller, *General Beck.*
53 On this topic see, in addition to the works of Deist and K.-J. Müller
    cited in note 6 above, H. Senff, 'Die Entwicklung der Panzerwaffe im
    deutschen Heer zwischen den beiden Weltkriegen', *Wehrwiss-
    enschaftliche Rundschau*, XIX, 1969, pp. 433–51 and 525–31 (also
    published separately, Frankfurt a. M., 1969) and Reynolds, *Beck*, p.
    91 ff and Karl Nehring, *Die Geschichte der deutschen Panzerwaffe*,
    Berlin, 1969. The works of Karl J. Walde, *Guderian. Eine Biographie*,
    Berlin, 1976, and Kenneth Mackesey, *Guderian. Der Panzergeneral*,
    Düsseldorf, 1976, again reflect Guderian's standpoint. See also
    Dermot Bradley, *Generaloberst Heinz Guderian und die
    Entstehungsgeschichte des modernen Blitzkrieges*, Osnabrück, 1978.
54 See his memorandum on 'Increasing the attacking Capability of the
    Army' of 30 December 1935: document 37 in K.-J. Müller, *General
    Beck.*
55 In his memorandum of 30 January 1936 on 'Tank Divisions and
    Motorised Troops' (document 39 in K.-J. Müller, *General Beck*) he
    energetically refuted the view that tanks ought to be used *only* as an
    auxiliary to the infantry, which was the view of the General Army
    Office.
56 Lecture of 15 February 1934 and memorandum of 9 May 1934 of
    Major-General Liese, Chief of the Army Arms Office, in
    Bundesarchiv-Militärarchiv, Wi F 5/1638; in the works cited in note
    6 above and in the following W. Deist sees, as does Geyer in the work
    cited in note 21, the fateful 'symbol of the whole of German
    rearmament after 1933' principally in this 'lack of closeness between
    the personnel and *matériel* components'. Quoted in *Francia*, V, 1977,
    p. 557.
57 Memorandum of the General Army Office (General Fromm) of 1
    August 1936 entitled 'Build-up of the Peacetime and Wartime Army'
    in Bundesarchiv-Militärarchiv, RH 15/v. 9; see also M. Geyer,
    'Militär, Rüstung and Aussenpolitik', p. 264 ff., and W. Deist,
    'Heeresrüstung und Aggression 1936–1939', published in the supple-
    ments to *Francia.*
58 Bundesarchiv-Militärarchiv, RH, 15/v. 9.
59 On this point see K.-J. Müller, *General Beck*, chapters VI and VII.
60 Up till now this fact has always been overlooked, even though it
    should have been noticed that although Beck may well have worded
    his biting criticism of Hitler's comments of 5 November 1937
    strongly, no criticism is known to have come from him of the revision
    of directives or additions to the directives which resulted from this

speech by Hitler. Part of the explanation may be due to the fact that he exerted decisive influence in revising the directives: K.-J. Müller, *General Beck*, chapter V.

61 *Ibid.*, chapters V and VI.

62 In addition to the reference cited in the previous note see especially Reynolds, *Beck*, chapters V and VI; K.-J. Müller, *Das Heer und Hitler*, chapters VII and VIII. Both also make use of older literature.

63 See document 55 in K.-J. Müller, *General Beck*.

64 The crucial memoranda and lecture notes are now printed in *ibid.*, documents 44 to 54.

65 More details on this in K.-J. Müller, *Das Heer und Hitler*, chapter VIII, and Reynolds, *Beck*, chapter VI.

66 Lecture note of 16 July 1938 (document 50 in K.-J. Müller, *General Beck*).

67 Beck's letter of 31 July 1938 to Lieutenant-General von Manstein (document 43 in K.-J. Müller, *Das Heer und Hitler*, p. 665); on Beck's relationship with Brauchitsch in 1938 see Hans Bernd Gisevius, *Bis zum bitteren Ende*, II, Darmstadt, 1947, pp. 18–20, and K.-J. Müller, *Das Heer und Hitler*, p. 337 ff.

68 See the account and references in K.-J. Müller, *General Beck*, chapter VI. On the British evaluation of the situation at that time in comparison with the German analysis: Donald Cameron Watt, *Too Serious a Business: European Armed Forces and the Approach to the Second World War*, London, 1975, p. 100 ff. For the assessment of the situation by the American military attaché see W. Deist, 'Berichte des US-Militärattachés in Berlin 1933–1939', in *Russland – Deutschland – Amerika. Festschrift für Fritz T. Epstein*, ed. A. Fischer, G. Moltmann and K. Schwabe, Wiesbaden, 1978, pp. 279–95.

69 References on the above in K.-J. Müller, *General Beck*, chapter VI. The analysis of summer 1937 is printed in H. Speidel, *Aus unserer Zeit*, pp. 431–53: 'Französischer Sicherheitsbegriff und französische Führung'.

70 Documents on the war game are to be found for the most part in Bundesarchiv-Militärarchiv, Wi/IF 5. 1502; see the analysis in K.-J. Müller, *General Beck*, chapter VI.

71 Beck on 16 November 1938 to Major Holtzmann: Bundesarchiv, Nachlass Holtzmann, No. 19 (document 55 in K.-J. Müller, *General Beck*).

The military opposition to Hitler
The problem of interpretation and analysis

I

Research on the German resistance has passed through several stages of development.

The central theme of the *first* phase was the strictly factual business of proving that an anti-Hitler opposition had existed, and the investigation of its activities, motives and ideas.[1] Here discussion centred on the problem of moral justification (particularly though not exclusively in relation to the military), especially in relation to the oath, or, as the case may be, the breaking of the oath, which was not a historical problem in the strictest sense. This type of approach, moreover, answered a politico-psychological need in view of the thesis of collective guilt which had been propagated abroad, and it also met certain of the legitimation needs of the new Federal Republic.

In the *second* stage of development historical research on the one hand placed the investigation of events in a more comprehensive framework and abandoned the narrow view which limited itself to the sequence of events on 20 July and the national-conservative opposition, so as to include opposition forces from very different social groups which defined themselves as being of a different political persuasion. On the other hand specialist research, in keeping with one of the larger questions of recent German history, took up the problem of continuity in connection with the phenomenon of the resistance.[2]

The *third* phase of development has long been characterised by the intensive effort to comprehend in conceptually adequate terms the phenomenon of the resistance, whose complexity has been made increasingly evident by research, and of finding an approach which would allow as comprehensive an historical explanation as possible.

Thanks to the results of recent research and the development of a theory of the Nazi regime, the lack of clarity, and the *a priori* nature, of the traditional concept of resistance have been well established.[3] The interpretation which thought to see in the resistance an autonomous and largely homogeneous phenomenon has seemed less and less appropriate, and the inadequacy of a view of the resistance which was determined mainly by political and moral considerations has become increasingly obvious. Recent research has for some time, therefore, focused on developing more extensive analytical and conceptual models which might provide a satisfactory alternative.[4]

To avoid possible misunderstandings what is in itself self-evident should at this point be re-emphasised. Such endeavours are not concerned to deny or even detract from the political and moral content of the uprising of 20 July 1944, or of those other resistance and opposition groups which did not belong to the national-conservative opposition, nor to deny, with the arrogance of those who come after, the fact that there *was* a serious opposition to Hitler.[5] They are concerned, rather, with the historically adequate analysis, by means of suitable conceptual and categorical references, of a phenomenon which has turned out to be more subtle, differentiated and problematic than earlier studies suggested. It is, furthermore, a question of research into the resistance keeping pace with the development of historical debate on Hitler's regime.

II

Ten years ago Hüttenberger put forward an important general approach to the categorical consideration of resistance and opposition, derived from games theory.[6] Resistance is understood here generally as a specific form of conflict within an asymmetrical relationship of rule, extending from nonconformist behaviour via deviant behaviour to civil disobedience, to conflicts inherent within the system and ultimately to conflicts which threaten to break it up. With this approach Hüttenberger succeeds in separating in a heuristically fruitful manner the levels of description and interpretation. In the case of the special subject area represented by the so-called 'military resistance', however, we can no longer remain on the purely formal level which Hüttenberger posits when he presents the 'resistance of the military' as 'resistance to constituent parts of the regime itself, turning against the dominant whole'.[7] This definition does indeed make it possible to break away from a global, dichotomous concept of resistance, and in my view it covers an essential aspect of the phenomenon. But in order to arrive at a differentiated description and a reasonably coherent explanation not only mere formal definitions are needed but also definitions of content.

Therefore a special approach to the historical phenomenon of the military opposition must be found which on the one hand puts it in a comprehensive, concrete, historical context and which, on the other is capable of analysing it with greater selectivity than Hüttenberger's general and formal model of 'resistance by parts of the whole against the dominant majority of that whole' allows. A concrete framework of historical reference must be put together which firstly does away with the idea of resistance as a dichotomous relationship between the 'system' and its 'opponents' and which secondly is able simultaneously to differentiate the model of 'part of the whole versus the dominant whole within a system'. This framework of reference must therefore include a number of different and variable elements.

Such an approach does not understand military resistance as part of a phenomenon which when added to other parts of the phenomenon such as Church resistance, workers' resistance, youth resistance, etc., constitutes the total phenomenon of 'resistance', so to speak, as a monolithic manifestation. Military resistance or military opposition is rather to be understood in the first place as a special case in the German military elite's relationship with the Nazi regime. Secondly, this relationship between the military and National Socialism is to be seen within the larger framework of the behaviour of traditional power elites in a political and social environment subject to far-reaching secular change.[8] Thus, from this viewpoint, the relationship of the military to the Nazi regime (including military opposition) is to be understood in relation to the symptoms of political and social change. Drawing on aspects of the theories both of Nazi rule and of modernisation, many complex aspects of the phenomenon of military opposition may firstly be classified qualitatively at a *descriptive* level and secondly, on an *explanatory* level, may be fitted into a historical context which is no longer of a political and moral nature.

III

The framework of historical reference can be outlined only very briefly here.[9] From about the second half of the nineteenth century the Prusso-German military elite as embodied in the officer caste had been insistently faced with two profound challenges. The first was the task of maintaining, or of establishing anew, its traditional political and social position in view of the radical change taking place in the world around it.

A purely functional role within the military apparatus was never the sum total of the position of the military elite in Prussia or later in Germany. That position was likewise more than mere social privilege. The military elite, given the traditions of the Prussian military state, enjoyed also a very considerable political importance. It was expressed in the claim, repeatedly and forcefully asserted, to a voice in political dialogue and decision-making. Sharing in power by participating in decision-making was an essential feature of the self-concept of this long-established officer class.[10]

The disintegration of the political and social structure, which had begun with the process of industrialisation and had been exacerbated by the world war, the upheaval in politics and the state, the great inflation and the economic crisis, intensified the challenge the military faced. Over and above this, the first world war had made the military elite aware of the second challenge confronting it. It had not only to face political and social change but also a far-reaching transformation in the business of warfare. Mechanised conflict between highly industrialised nations represented for the traditional officer caste and their outlook just as powerful a menace as changes in politics and society. Now new sources of tension were manifesting themselves in dichotomies such as traditional serving officers *v.* the mechanised army, or the exclusive military caste *v.* the modern mass army, or military professionalism *v.* mobilisation of the whole of society.[11]

This complicated situation, in which political and social change had combined with the revolution in the means of waging war to form a formidable threat to its position, elicited a variety of responses from the officer corps. All the differing opinions on how it could best maintain its standing can, however, be reduced to a single basic model. This was the view that these two crucial issues could only be resolved in the long term if, firstly, the structure of the state were remodelled along authoritarian lines, and secondly, if a new legitimating basis among the mass of the populace were secured for the groups constituting the traditional elite. This is, so to speak, the common denominator to which the different views among the officer class, which at times were in quite sharp conflict, can be reduced. Those who were concerned primarily to reinforce their political and social influence and those who regarded the optimisation of the military machine and its technology as a prerequisite for maintaining their traditional power base were in agreement on both points.[12]

Such agreement was also the basis on which the consensus about the long-term political objectives of the traditional military elite rested. These can likewise be summarised in two points. The first is the restoration of the Reich's standing as a great power, which had been lost in the war. This status as a great power was defined chiefly in military terms and in terms of power politics.[13] The second point is the complete organisation, conceived and directed by the military leadership, of the whole nation, in view of the pitch modern warfare had reached, which, under the conditions of an industrial era, was defined as 'total'.[14]

The idea of solving these two central sets of problems, together with the realisation of these two objectives, formed the three essential elements which constituted the political programme of the German officer caste.

Up to 1933 several alternative strategies for realising this concept had either failed or proved impracticable. This is true of the putsch strategy of the group around General von Lüttwitz (1920);[15] it is also true in the final analysis of Seeckt's policy (1920–26),[16] which could not have lasted for any length of time, and it is true of the alternatives to Seeckt developed by Groener and Schleicher (1926–33).[17] Those high-ranking officers who since January 1933 had gained decisive influence in the armed forces command, therefore, thought the proper solution was to be found in a coalition of the national-conservative and German national forces with the leadership of the National Socialist movement, such as emerged on 30 January 1933 in the shape of Hitler's Cabinet, especially as a prominent position was reserved for the armed forces in this *rapprochement*.[18] Hitler's formula of twin pillars on which the new regime would rest – the army and the party – bore the hallmark of tactical skill and was carefully designed to meet the expectations of the military.

The traditional military elite, as a secondary system within the political and social structure, had not, on its own, been in a position to create for itself an adequate basis of legitimation for action in a phase of rapid political, social and technological change. In the view of the representatives of the military elite the 'entente' of influential groups among the traditional German elites with the leadership of the Nazi movement, as epitomised by Hitler's Cabinet in January 1933, promised to achieve such a basis.[19] It seemed to grant the conditions for the realisation of the three essential objectives already mentioned. The first objective concerned *domestic* policy. It was the re-establishment and securing of the military elite's traditional position of power in the state and in society, a position at risk ever since 1918. The second lay in the area of *foreign* policy, namely the restoration of the Reich to the position of a world power, defined in military and political terms. The third objective, closely linked with the second, was one of *military* policy. It sought the permanent war mobilisation of the whole of society, summed up in the euphemism 'making the nation capable of defending itself', as a necessary condition of great-power status. Such preparedness for war was regarded as an inescapable require-ment, given the demands of an industrial and technological era.

These objectives became articles of faith in the military's rela-tionship with the National Socialist regime. The course of that relationship was markedly determined by the degree to which it promised to realise the hopes the military elite had pinned on the *rapprochement*. That is to say, it was heavily influenced by whether the aspirations defined in the three basic objectives indicated above were helped, hindered or even queried. In concrete terms it meant that relations between the military and the regime warmed or cooled in the following way:

1. In *domestic policy*, according to the extent to which the armed forces' claim to a position of equal power in the state was admitted or disputed.
2. In the area of *foreign policy*, according to the extent to which the aspiration to great-power status, defined in terms of power politics and military strength, was accepted and promoted or endangered.

3.   As far as the *total organisation of the nation* for war readiness
     was concerned, according to the guaranteeing of the military
     command's determining role in the process and the realisation
     of its conception of the methods to be used.

IV

The framework outlined above affords a suitable basic interpretative model allowing more precise historical definition of the
phenomenon of military opposition or military resistance. Historically it is thus to be defined as a phenomenon complementary to the
rapprochement of the traditional elite cadres with Hitler and his
movement. Military opposition and military resistance, therefore,
are a complex phenomenon of conflict within the framework of
that *rapprochement*.

Moreover, this also enables us to differentiate between the
resistance of '*a priori* opponents', that is, of opposition forces
whose own self-concept, and that of the Nazis, allowed of no
shades of grey between opposition, neutrality or coalition.[20]

In order to derive an adequate *descriptive* model appropriate to
the complexity of the phenomenon from such an *explanatory* one,
certain additional elements of differentiation and analysis need to
be introduced. Only then can the phenomenon of conflict be
described adequately in all its diffuseness, from alternative positions inherent within the system to alternative positions which
sought to overcome it. Certain difficulties, even absurdities, in
previous attempts at understanding can then be resolved and the
reactions of the military elite to a variety of challenges explained.
What are these additional categories?

Firstly, the question of conflict should be analysed from the
standpoint of which of the three essential objectives — the alliance
character of the *rapprochement*, the foreign-policy concept of
great-power status, or the mobilisation of the whole of society —
individually or together seemed, in the opinion of the leading
military figures, to be questioned or threatened. A line of enquiry
based on these three fundamental objectives allows something that
other interpretative approaches have not so far achieved: credible
explanation of why it was that the more notorious practices and
principles of the regime aroused unease and adverse comment in
military circles (such as, for example, the early liquidation of

political and ideological opponents, or antisemitic measures which were blatantly in violation not only of the law but of common humanity)[21] whereas, on the other hand, only risky ventures on the international scene or Röhm's military ambitions or the plot against Fritsch gave rise to politically significant protest. Such questions can be resolved within the interpretative framework outlined, in conjunction with the additional element of analysis mentioned above. The repression of political opponents did not affect the three basic objectives in any degree; the last-mentioned cases did. Thus in summer 1934,[22] just as in the Fritsch crisis of 1938,[23] the very foundations of the *rapprochement* seemed to be in serious danger. Leading figures on the general staff saw Germany's prospects of becoming a great power threatened repeatedly by Hitler's policy: Beck saw it in the Sudetenland crisis;[24] after the Polish campaign Halder saw it in the continuation and expansion of hostilities as a result of Hitler's plans for an offensive in the west.[25] Later attempts to bring the war to an end in order to rescue the German people and the German state from certain disaster are likewise to be subsumed under this count.[26] Further more, it can be added that the strategy of permanent war mobilisation which earned the antagonism of the Chief of the War Economy Office, General Thomas, and other officers became a matter of controversy thanks to some of Hitler's decisions on economic and rearmament policy and to rivalries between military men and other groups in the regime.[27]

The question as to which of the three fundamental objectives appeared threatened is, however, to be supplemented by a *second* question. From whom and in what way did the threat of interference arise, at least in the eyes of the military? Here is thus a matter of weighing up the opposition.

This issue, which also includes the difficult problem of just how the military elite perceived the world around it, makes it possible to describe and explain in precise terms the range of reaction in situations of conflict. A development can thus be traced, for instance, in terms of the military elite defensively protecting its own position, then offensively stabilising it (e.g. under the rubric of 'purging the Reich of "radical" elements'), to planning and attempting to overthrow the system. From this point of view it was of considerable importance to ascertain whether, as the leading members of the military elite saw it, the basic objectives were definitely being threatened or at any rate contested by, for instance, individual personalities or groups within the Nazi movement or by Hitler himself. This fact decisively influenced the nature of the reaction.

Here are three instances, each case reflecting a different conjuncture of events.

1.   The first is the quarrel with the SA which culminated in the Röhm affair.[28] Why did the horrific way in which the SA leadership was eliminated, and the cold-blooded murder of figures critical of the regime — among them two former generals (their colleagues) — not evoke any politically significant reaction in the officer corps, or at least among those who claimed to speak for it?

Within the framework of the intepretative model outlined above there can be only one answer. In the eyes of the armed forces command Röhm's policy with the first serious threat to the army's position within the Reich as monopoly wielder of the state's means of power and as one of the twin pillars of the regime. On several fronts the aspirations of Röhm and his SA thus jeopardised the arrangement of 1933. Hitler, on the other hand, proved himself as it were a loyal coalition partner when with his brutal initiative against the SA leadership he stabilised the 'twin pillar' set-up against those among the Nazi movement who sought to overturn it. From this viewpoint the complaisance over mass murder, the readiness to support Hitler as Hindenburg's successor, the oath of loyalty to Hitler, all become explicable. In the eyes of the overwhelming majority of the officer corps Hitler remained the trusty coalition partner in the face of dangerous elements within the National Socialist movement.

2.   The second example is afforded by the conflicts between the army[29] and the representatives and organs of the party, especially the SS, in the years 1934 to 1937–38. These conflicts, which were at times bitter, did not lead to a reaction on the part of the military such as to destabilise the system. The explanation is likewise obvious in the light of our categorical framework. As the leading military personnel saw it, neither the fighting services' monopoly of armed force nor their constitutive role in the regime were openly in jeopardy.[30] But, above all, in this conflict Hitler seemed to the leaders of the military to be acting in the capacity of mediator, as a fair-minded arbiter who was disposed favourably towards the army and who was trying to bring the regime's warring factions to settle

their differences and co-operate with one another. If he no longer appeared as a partner and ally in these disputes, he did not appear as an opponent, either. The 'articles of faith' of the 1933 accommodation with the Nazis was still, therefore, it seemed being safeguarded here, not least through Hitler's supposed efforts to achieve a settlement.[31]

3. The third example is the Fritsch-Blomberg crisis.[32] The situation the generals faced here was no longer so clear-cut. It was primarily Himmler, Heydrich, the Gestapo and the SS, with Goering active behind the scenes, who had struck a treacherous blow against the army with the plot against Fritsch. Many interested parties found Hitler's behaviour disturbing; at least perplexing. The solution he finally imposed put paid to the idea of him as an arbitrator favourable to the army, especially since the organisational changes he ordered seemed at best double-edged.[33] For several key figures in the later resistance the Fritsch crisis marked, therefore, a distinct turning-point, as Graml has shown in the case of General Oster,[34] for example, and Scheurig in the case of Tresckow.[35] At the time these two officers suggested moves for an internal purge of the regime which amounted to offensive measures to stabilise the army's position within it — measures which would naturally have altered the regime's character.[36]

In these three instances the sole factor influencing the nature and strength of the army's reaction was whether and how far its position within the regime was threatened. This, and not considerations of morality, was the heart of the matter. The officer corps may well have been loud in its moral condemnation but in each case it was issues of power politics that were the motivating factor, and, for the military men concerned, so much was brought out in the role Hitler played in these affairs.

A *third element* which should be brought in to complete the descriptive framework outlined above can be adumbrated as the question of the order of priorities among these aims. There were diverging views within the military elite on the relative importance of each of the three basic objectives. The allocation of priorities to the projected aims of the military elite was of possible decisive importance in determining its attitude to the regime in general and the nature and speed of its reaction to cases of conflict in particular. Various factors, such as the specific interests of departments, or different views of the role of the military, affected the degree of emphasis. In a case of conflict a 'modern' technical specialist concerned primarily to optimise the effectiveness of the military machine would, without question, emphasise different priorities from those of an officer who stood by the older tradition of claims to a political and social role. It also depended very substantially on the assessment of the actual or supposed symmetry or asymmetry between the army's objectives and those of the Nazis.[37] Here the borderline was often far from clear and liable to change anyway, the more so as departmental interests altered with the needs of the moment, and technological progressiveness could coexist with insistence on traditional status.[38]

The *fourth* element to be considered within the descriptive and explanatory framework is closely connected with the question of priority among the basic objectives. It concerns the alternative strategies designed to realise the projected goals. There were considerably divergent views about how best to bring the objectives about in practice, and they strongly influenced the development of relations between the military and the regime, provoking a change of stance from deviant behaviour to resistance which destabilised the regime.

The contrast in approach between Reichenau, who, as head of the Armed Forces Office, saw the consolidation of the army's position in Hitler's state best guaranteed by an open policy, willing to embrace new departures, and Fritsch,[39] who preferred to reach the same end by clinging to traditional values and patterns of behaviour, was of considerable importance for the military elite's attitude to the regime and for the determination of the point at which, so to speak, the *modus vivendi* of 1933 broke down. Such a divergence in styles was ultimately to have political consequences and it was at the root of the long-standing controversy between the Supreme Command of the Armed Forces and the army general staff over the organisation of the highest military echelon.[40] It was no coincidence that the conspirators of 20 July 1944 had prepared a decree changing the top military command structure.[41]

V

In view of the complexity of the historical phenomenon of military opposition the elements of analysis just laid out are fundamental, necessary components of any differentiated descriptions and of any historically adequate consideration of the subject as a whole. The political path of the Chief of the General Staff of the army, Ludwig Beck, offers a good example of how markedly the progress from approval of the regime to becoming the central figure of the resistance was influenced by factors such as the conflicts of aims, the perception of opponents, and alternative strategies.[42]

All these factors are to be found playing a part in Beck's quarrel with Hitler over the Czech question early in summer of 1938. The considerations we have mentioned allow the incident to be broken down analytically and they also allow the separate stages in the development of the conflict to be described in a differentiated way. First of all, it was a disagreement over *methods*, behind which was a conflict about *roles*. That is to say, it was principally a question of divergent views of the military command's role within the regime. Hitler assigned it a purely instrumental role, that of the realisation by the military of his political decisions. Beck, on the other hand, laid claim to the equal right of responsible military officers to share in discussions and decision-making in questions of military and foreign policy.[43] From this standpoint he criticised Hitler's methods of arriving at decisions, which was in direct opposition to his own view of the role of the military command: basic political decisions had been taken in 'a solitary act of decision-making' by the Führer alone, without consulting those in positions of military responsibility. In this dispute over procedure Beck tried at first to clarify the situation by memoranda, that is, by working from within the system.

The conflict of 1938 was, however, at the same time also about *strategy*. Like Hitler, Beck was convinced that, as he himself wrote,[44] the continued existence of Czechoslovakia 'in its present form' was 'intolerable' for Germany. The Masaryks' republic had to be eliminated as a factor in power politics. The conflict with Hitler was therefore not about objectives but about the appropriate strategy for achieving them. Hitler wanted an immediate, direct military intervention. Beck, on the other hand, wanted to wait for the point in time which was most favourable as regards the state of rearmament, foreign affairs and military policy. If possible, he would have avoided the direct use of military force. Hence, in this case there was a fundamental difference less about the objective than about the strategy to be adopted. Beck sought to resolve this conflict over strategy by means of debate which were within the bounds of the system and which went as far as the threat of resignation.

Beyond a certain point this cluster of disagreements developed into a fundamental conflict about aims which affected at least one of the three basic objectives in a crucial way. Beck saw in Hitler's adherence to the intention of invading at the time he alone had decided, against the advice of the Chief of the General Staff, a hazardous policy which involved a serious risk to Germany's chances of becoming a great power in the future. To Beck's way of thinking the objective of 'Germany achieving great-power status' took priority in this situation over the internal harmony of the entente between army and regime.[45] At first he tried to resolve matters by applying such pressure as the system allowed (collective resignation of the most senior generals). In the process, however, his 'perception of his opponent' underwent a change.

If in spring and early summer 1938 he had still thought that radical forces in the party, the very ones which had already set afoot the plot against Fritsch, were the warmongers in Hitler's *entourage*, he had subsequently to recognise that in the last analysis it was Hitler himself who was the author of the dangerous policy of using war to secure his ends. In realising this, however, he had reached the threshold separating *conflicts*, inherent in the system, about methods, roles, strategy and aims, from *resistance which would destabilise the regime*.

By means of the categories cited and applied here an analysis can be undertaken, analogous to that of the Chief of the General Staff's progress, of the paths to resistance taken by other members of the officer corps who differed considerably from Beck in age, background and career. In this analysis, however, attention will be focused not on individuals but on revealing whether, and if so to what extent, our categorical model is adequate in a comparison of types within the interpretative framework used. For this purpose a brief reference to the changing attitude of Henning von Tresckow, one of the central figures of the military resistance during the war, may suffice. Despite his reservations about domestic policy on account of Nazi intrigues (for example, in the area of religious policy), Tresckow had approved of the oath to Hitler in 1934. At that time he placed the *rapprochement* higher among his priorities than the less attractive face of the regime.[46] Two years later he called for the army to take steps against the SS and Gestapo at the same time as he was working intensively on the plans for deployment against Czechoslovakia. With regard to German ambitions to regain the status of a great power he was in sympathy with the regime.[47] At this stage he saw the army's position jeopardised by the SS and Gestapo, but not by the regime's totalitarian claims, and therefore advised, as he did during the Fritsch crisis, that the army should maintain an offensive stance.[48] Then in 1938–39 anxiety not to set the great-power objective at risk outweighed his predisposition towards the entente arrangement: war must be avoided, since it could not be won. Hitler, the dancing dervish, must be shot dead.[49] These were strong words from a junior member of the general staff, but above all they reflect a clear assignment of priorities. Sustaining the objective of securing Germany's place among the great nations of Europe was more important to him than sustaining the system. Consistent with this, but conversely, he was once again enthusiastic for a while after the fall of France in 1940, hoping that the war could now be ended on the basis of power which the Reich had won.[50] The system had evidently not imperilled Germany's future. Then, with the Russian campaign, he saw catastrophe looming for a regime whose criminal character had become plain to him in the meantime (the Barbarossa orders and the Commissar orders). The way to planning a *coup d'état* lay open.[51]

Thus the example of Tresckow shows that, within the framework of the interpretative approach outlined above, the movement towards participation in the military resistance can be broken down analytically, described with some discrimination and at the same time explained in all its individual stages by means of the categories of *prioritising the objectives, alternative strategies, the perception of opponents* and the *difference over methods*. It also shows the extent to which the exercise is possible over and above considerations of individual personality factors. The network of categories outlined above allows more than a mere schematisation of events and developments to be adduced. It permits of a sensitivity of analysis such that one can probe in more precise terms a complex phenomenon like resistance within the military without exposing oneself to the difficulties of the customary, all too diffuse, concept of resistance. Furthermore, it offers a basis for classifying this phenomenon in an *historical interpretative framework* which no longer has to have recourse to the moral and political categories which in the past have been typical of so many efforts at understanding.

This is not in any sense to detract from the vital role played by moral and ethical considerations as an influence on the various historical manifestations of opposition and resistance. In the sources they confront us explicitly and strikingly. Indeed, they are found not merely as an element of justification after the failure of the attempted *coup*, but also in many another train of events long before 1944. The problem is that ethical and moral considerations were never changeless absolute and never a universal factor common to all the cases which occurred. What can be shown to have had an ethical and moral 'effect' on one person may not have had the same influence on others. On the other hand moral outrage and a feeling that something was objectionable on ethical grounds did not always provoke repercussions in the sense of politically significant opposition or even resistance. There remains, therefore, the difficulty of explaining why it was so in any particular case: why moral revulsion should have led in one instance to action of the nature of political opposition, but not in another; why such feelings should have arisen on one occasion, but not on another.

If we are not to dispose of these problems by attempting to explain them away in terms of individual personality — a method ill befitting the accepted standards of historical enquiry — then we must first determine the content, causes and timing of the moral and ethical considerations. For example, in spring 1934 Colonel (later Field-Marshal) Manstein of the general staff objected in a detailed memorandum[52] to the dismissal of soldiers of Jewish extraction with, *inter alia*, a reference to 'the moral aspect'. Careful examination of his arguments shows that the word 'moral' here referred to the exclusive and limited group morality of an autonomous, self-regulating officer corps. At the time Manstein thought this specific, particularist morality was affected by the racist measures which had been ordered; the general moral problem of racial sanctions had no bearing on the case at all.[53] But his case too can be subsumed without much difficulty under one of the categories mentioned above, that of the internally autonomous standing of the army.

Other examples, among them the deep moral indignation of Major Stieff[54] or of Lieutenant-Colonel Gersdorff[55] at the mass murders perpetrated in Poland and Russia by the Security Service's task forces — the SD-Einsatzgruppen — show that revulsion of a pre-eminently moral nature had evidently to be augmented by some further signal impulse or impulses before the crucial step to politically relevant opposition was taken. Such an impulse might have come, for instance, from an insight into the operational planning and conduct of the war, characterised by military experts as irresponsible, or it might derive simply from contact, in the course of official duties, or in a relationship of trust established socially, with comrades and superiors[56] who for their part had already made, mentally at least, the break with the regime.

These and other examples indicate sufficiently that moral indignation or rejection of the regime on ethical and moral grounds did not in itself automatically evince a specifically political opposition or even one that had political repercussions. Further motivating factors had always to be added or to have been already experienced. But, as studies of the development of important representatives of the military opposition available to us prove, these were of such a nature that they can be considered without difficulty within the descriptive categories we have developed and can thus be made explicable. Such motivating factors might be, for instance, a fundamental threat to objectives in foreign policy and/or to a man's views on the internal political structure or to his own interests.[57]

Conversely this is also true for the cases of those military men who, each faced with the decision from his own particular position, felt they could not take the fatal step into opposition despite grave doubts about the morality of the regime. The conduct of Beck's successor, General Halder, in the winter of 1939–40 shows this clearly. In the last analysis, apart from the technical and personnel problems of a *coup*, which should not be understated, two factors held the Chief of the General Staff back from such a move. One was his calculation, based seemingly on reason, of the success of a large-scale offensive against the Western powers which, he thought, would make a victorious end to the war possible. The other was his conviction that the overthrow of the Western allies could bring about the realisation of the foreign-policy objective of attaining the position for the Reich of a great power.[58]

The many aspects of motivation subsumed under the concept of the moral and the ethical are not, therefore, to be regarded solely as a subjective factor, and, so to speak, important for individual biographies. Rather, they assume a general quality and are to be understood as a constituent part of a position of antagonism to the regime. As such they can be categorised only by an analysis of their content and historical causes, beyond any attempt to understand the psychology of the individual. But in this way they can be considered and delineated in categories, according to their origin and structure, and can be interpreted historically on a supra-individual basis. A concept of the resistance as it is traditionally understood in terms of moral criteria would not have the heuristic scope and selectivity necessary for this.[59]

A differentiated *description* and an historical *explanation* of the multifarious, complex reactions of the German military elite to the challenge it faced from the politics and nature of the Nazi regime therefore require a comprehensive classificatory and interpretative approach which goes well beyond that traditional concept of resistance. The preceding pages are meant to offer a stimulus and a basis for discussion of the problem.

Notes

This is a revised version of a lecture given on 5 October 1978 at the thirty-second Historians' Conference in Hamburg. Since then the discussion has been pushed further. Cf. the book edited by Jürgen Schmädeke and Peter Steinbach, *Der Widerstand gegen den Nationalsozialismus. Die deutsche Gesellschaft und der Widerstand gegen Hitler*, Munich, 1985, which resumes the present state of the debate.

1   Cf. the special biographies by U. Hochmuth, *Faschismus und Widerstand. Ein Verzeichnis deutschsprachiger Literatur*, Frankfurt a. M., 1973, and R. Büchel, *Der deutsche Widerstand im Spiegel von Fachliteratur und Publizistik seit 1945*, Munich, 1975; latest, comprehensive bibliography: Ulrich Cantarius (*ed.*), *Bibliographie 'Widerstand'*, Munich, New York, London and Paris, 1984; also G. R. Ueberschär, 'Gegner des Nationalsozialismus 1933–45. Volksopposition, individuelle Gewissensentscheidung und Rivalitätskampf konkurrierender Führungseliten als Aspekte der Literatur über Emigration and Widerstand', *Militärgeschichtliche Mitteilungen*, 35, 1984, pp. 141–96. A detailed survey of the historiographical positions and on all main aspects of resistance is. Klaus-Jürgen Müller (*ed*)., *Der deutsche Widerstand 1933–1945*, Paderborn, 1986. The state of debate in the German Democratic Republic is represented by Klaus Mammach, *Die deutsche antifaschistische Widerstandsbewegung 1933–1939*, (East) Berlin, 1974.

2   Representative works on the one side would be: Bodo Scheurig, *Freies Deutschland. Das Nationalkomitee und der Bund Deutscher Offiziere*

in der Sowjetunion 1943–1945, 2nd edn., 1967; Heinz Höhne, *Kennwort 'Direktor'. Die Geschichte der Roten Kapelle*, 1970; Hans-Josef Steinberg. *Widerstand und Verfolgung in Essen 1933 bis 1945*, 1969, and Kurt Klotzbach, *Gegen den Nationalsozialismus. Widerstand und Verfolgung in Dortmund 1930–1945. Eine historisch-politische Studie*, 1969; on the other: Hans Mommsen, 'Gesellschaftsbild und Verfassungspläne des deutschen Widerstandes', and Hermann Graml, 'Die aussenpolitischen Vorstellungen des deutschen Widerstandes', both in *Der deutsche Widerstand gegen Hitler. Vier historisch-kritische Studien*, ed. Walter Schmitthenner and Hans Buchheim, Cologne and Berlin, 1966.

3 See Peter Hüttenberger, 'Die nationalsozialistische Polykratie', in *Das nationalsozialistische Herrschaftsystem*, ed. Heinrich August Winkler (Geschichte und Gesellschaft, No. 4, 1974), with a survey of the most important literature on the structure of Nazi rule; in addition: Hans Mommsen, 'Nationalsozialismus', in *Sowjetsytem und Demokratische Gesellschaft*, IV, Freiburg, Basle and Vienna, 1971; Wolfgang J. Mommsen, 'Das nationalsozialistische Herrschaftssystem', *Jahrbuch der Universität Düsseldorf*, 1970/71.

4 On this point see the observations in R. Mann, 'Widerstand gegen des Nationalsozialismus', *Neue Politische Literatur*, XXII, 1977, pp. 425–42; the approach determined by politico-ethical and personal considerations has recently appeared again in Peter Hoffmann, *Widerstand gegen Hitler. Probleme des Umsturzes*, Munich, 1979.

5 Erdmann's criticism of the position presented in what follows could be understood in this way: Gebhardt, *Handbuch der Deutschen Geschichte*, IV/2, 9th edn., Stuttgart, 1976, p. 483, n. 13.

6 P. Hüttenberger, 'Vorüberlegungen zum "Widerstandsbegriff"', in *Theorien in der Praxis des Historikers*, ed. Jürgen Kocka (Geschichte und Gesellschaft, No. 3, 1977).

7 Hüttenberger, 'Widerstandsbegriff', p. 133.

8 Cf. K.-J. Müller, 'Ludwig Beck – Probleme seiner Biographie', *Militärgeschichtliche Mitteilungen*, XI, 1972, p. 167 ff.

9 See the thoughtful survey by Michael Geyer, 'Die Geschichte des deutschen Militärs von 1860 bis 1945', in *Die moderne deutsche Geschichte in der internationalen Forschung 1945–1975* (Geschichte und Gesellschaft, No. 4, 1978), and Wolfgang Sauer, 'Die politische Geschichte der deutschen Armee und das Problem des Militarismus', *Politische Vierteljahresschrift*, VI, 1965.

10 See the first chapter of the present volume, this and also Manfred Messerschmidt, *Militär und Politik in der Bismarckzeit und im Wilhelminischen Deutschland*, Darmstadt, 1975 (Erträge der Forschung, 43), and *id.*, 'Werden und Prägung des deutschen Offizierkorps', in *Offiziere im Bild von Dokumenten aus drei Jahrhunderten*, Stuttgart, 1964. See also Martin Kitchen, *The German Officer Corps 1890–1914*, Oxford, 1973; Hermann Rumschöttel, *Das bayerische Offizierkorps 1866–1914*, Berlin, 1973; Holger H. Herwig, *The German Naval Officer Corps: a Social and Political History, 1890–*

1918, Oxford, 1973.

11   Michael Geyer develops this viewpoint into a comprehensive frame
     of reference in his standard work, *Aufrüstung oder Sicherheit. Die
     Reichswehr und die Krise der Machtpolitik 1924–1936*, Wiesbaden,
     1980.

12   M. Geyer, 'Die Geschichte des deutschen Militärs', p. 273 ff., with
     references to the most recent literature, and Andreas Hillgruber,
     'Militarismus am Ende der Weimarer Republik', in *id.*, *Grossmacht-
     politik und Militarismus im zwanzigsten Jahrhundert. Drei Beiträge
     zum Kontinuitätsproblem*, Düsseldorf, 1974, pp. 37–51.

13   A. Hillgruber, 'Kontinuität und Diskontinuität in der deutschen
     Aussenpolitik', in *ibid.*, pp. 11–36.

14   Berenice A. Caroll, *Design for Total War: Arms and Economics in
     the Third Reich*, The Hague and Paris, 1968, and the work by M.
     Geyer cited in note *id.*, 'Der zur Organisation erhobene
     Burgfrieden', in K.-J. Müller and Eckardt Opitz (eds.), *Militär und
     Militarismus in der Weimarer Republik*, Düsseldorf, 1978, p. 15 ff.;
     Ernst Willi Hansen, *Reichswehr und Industrie. Rüstungswirtschaftli-
     che Zusammenarbeit und wirtschaftliche Mobilmachungsvor-
     bereitung 1923–1932*, Boppard, 1978 (Wehrwissenschaftliche
     Forschung/Abt. Militärgeschichtliche Studien, 24). See also the
     critical bibliographical survey by M. Geyer, 'Die Wehrmacht der
     Deutschen Republik ist die Reichswehr. Bemerkungen zur neueren
     Literatur', *Militärgeschichtliche Mitteilungen*, XIV, 1973, p. 151.

15   Johannes Erger, *Der Kapp-Lüttwitz-Putsch. Ein Beitrag zur deut-
     schen Innenpolitik 1919/20*, Düsseldorf, 1967 (Beiträge zur Geschi-
     chte des Parlamentarismus und der politischen Parteien, 35); referen-
     ces to further writing in M. Geyer, 'Die Wehrmacht', p. 161.

16   Hans Meier-Welcker, *Seeckt*, Frankfurt a. M., 1967; Carl Guske,
     *Das politische Denken des Generals von Seeckt. Ein Beitrag zur
     Diskussion des Verhältnisses Seeckt-Reichswehr-Republik*, Lüb-
     eck and Hamburg, 1971.

17   In addition to the works by A. Hillgruber and M. Geyer cited in
     notes 11 and 12 above see also the works on Schleicher mentioned in
     n.31 of the first chapter of the present volume.

18   K.-J. Müller, *Das Heer und Hitler. Armee und national-sozialistis-
     ches Regime 1933–1940*, Stuttgart, 1969 (Beiträge zur Militär- und
     Kriegsgeschichte, 10).

19   *Ibid.* p. 35 ff.

20   Reference should be made here first to the groups whom the Nazi
     ideology of race left no possibility of choice, that is, primarily the
     Jews, followed by those who had no option for religious or
     ideological reasons, such as for instance representatives of a Christian
     fundamentalism, and finally to the supporters of political movements
     which, like the communists and anarchists, opposed the existing
     social and state order on principle.

21   See, for example, the reaction in military circles to the introduction
     of the so-called 'Aryan paragraph' in the armed forces: K.-J. Müller,

Das Heer und Hitler, p. 78 ff., and M. Messerschmidt, *Die Wehr-macht im NS-Staat. Zeit der Indoktrination*, Hamburg, 1969, p. 40 ff.

22 On the 'Röhm affair' see K.-J. Müller, *Das Heer und Hitler*, chapter III, and *id.*, 'Reichswehr und "Röhmaffäre"', *Militärgeschichtliche Mitteilungen*, III, 1968, pp. 107–44.

23 K.-J. Müller, *Das Heer und Hitler*, chapter IV, (the Blomberg scandal and the Fritsch crisis), and Harold C. Deutsch, *Hitler and his Generals: the Hidden Crisis, January–June 1938*, Minneapolis and London, 1974.

24 For different interpretations of this see Wolfgang Foerster, *Generaloberst Ludwig Beck. Sein Kampf gegen den Krieg*, Munich, 1953; Nicholas Reynolds, *Treason was no Crime: Ludwig Beck, Chief of General Staff*, London, 1976, and K.-J. Müller, *General Ludwig Beck. Studien und Dokumente zur politisch-militärischen Vorstellungswelt und beruflichen Tätigkeit des Generalstabschefs des deutschen Heeres 1933 bis 1938*, Boppard, 1980.

25 Harold C. Deutsch, *The Conspiracy against Hitler in the Twilight War*, London and Minneapolis, 1968, and K.-J. Müller, *Das Heer und Hitler*, chapter IX.

26 P. Hoffmann, *The History of the German Resistance, 1933–45*, London, 1977, and Bernd Martin, *Friedensinitiativen und Machtpolitik im Zweiten Weltkrieg 1939–1942*, Düsseldorf, 1974.

27 Cf. Georg Thomas, *Geschichte der deutschen Wehr- und Rüstungswirtschaft (1918–1943/45)*, ed. Wolfgang Birkenfeld, Boppard, 1966 (Schriften des Bundesarchivs, 14); also B. A. Caroll, *Design for Total War* (see note 14); and Timothy W. Mason, *Arbeiterklasse und Volksgemeinschaft. Dokumente und Materialien zur deutschen Arbeiterpolitik 1936–1939*, Opladen, 1975.

28 In addition to the literature cited in note 22 see Charles Bloch, *Die SA und die Krise des NS-Regimes 1934*, Frankfurt, 1970; Heinrich Bennecke, *Die Reichswehr und der 'Röhm-Putsch'*, Munich, 1962, and the personal account of F. G. von Tschirschky, *Erinnerungen eines Hochverräters*, Stuttgart, 1972.

29 K.-J. Müller, *Das Heer und Hitler*, chapter IV, and *id.*, *Ludwig Beck*, chapter II.

30 This is also expressed indirectly in Fritsch's words: 'Quite independently of the fact that the foundation of our army today is and must be National Socialist, the penetration of party influences into the army cannot be tolerated': record of 1 February 1938, printed in Friedrich Hossbach, *Zwischen Wehrmacht und Hitler*, Wolfenbüttel, Hanover, 1949, p. 70.

31 See Hitler's emphatic declaration of trust in the 'Reichswehr' at the New Year reception of 1935 and his speech to leading representatives of the party and the armed forces on 3 January 1935 (K.-J. Müller, *Das Heer und Hitler*, p. 158 f.) and General von Fritsch's comments to the commanders in chief of the armed forces of 12 January 1935 (Bundesarchiv-Militärarchiv, WK VII/1343, file 13) and in his memorandum of 1 February 1938 (F. Hossbach, *Zwischen Wehr-*

macht und Hitler, p. 69 ff.). The General believed that Hitler was 'totally disposed towards the armed forces' (12 January 1935) and had declared his 'absolute belief in the army's loyalty' in this conflict (2 January 1938).

32   See the literature cited in note 23 above.

33   On the reaction in army command circles see K.-J. Müller, *Das Heer und Hitler*, chapter VI.

34   H. Graml, 'Der Fall Oster', *Vierteljahrshefte für Zeitgeschichte*, XIV, 1966. At the time General Beck noted down as the impression of attitudes within the officer corps that the Fritsch case 'had opened up an unbridgable gulf between Hitler and the officer corps, even in relation to the question of mutual trust.' Bundesarchiv-Militärarchiv, N 28/3, note of 29 July 1938.

35   B. Scheurig, *Henning von Tresckow. Eine Biographie*, 3rd edn., Hamburg, 1973.

36   B. Scheurig, p. 56 ff.: at that time Tresckow, along with a regimental fellow officer under the Berlin military district commander, General von Witzleben, had called for steps to be taken to purge the regime, that is, military action to effect a transformation of the system.

37   The activity of some officers in the Intelligence Department shows, for example, how the lines could become blurred between the aggressive policy of conquest, which they rejected, and the national-conservative aspirations to a position as a great power, which they approved. Groscurth, for instance, controlled the 'nationality policy' in the Sudetenland and in the (then) western areas of Poland during the preparatory phase of Nazi expansion against Czechoslovakia and Poland. See Helmuth Groscurth, *Tagebücher eines Abwehroffiziers, 1938–1940*, ed. Helmut Krausnick and Harold C. Deutsch, Stuttgart, 1970 (Quellen und Darstellungen zur Zeitgeschichte, 19).

38   In this context a comparative analysis of the contemporary notes of high-ranking military officers would be informative, as, for instance, of G. Thomas (see note 27), H. Groscurth (note 37), Helmut Stieff, 'Ausgewählte Briefe, *Vierteljahrshefte für Zeitgeschichte*, II, 1954, pp. 291–332; Eduard Wagner, *Der Generalquartiermeister. Briefe und Tagebuchaufzeichnungen des Generalquartiermeisters des Heeres, General der Artillerie Eduard Wagner*, ed. Elisabeth Wagner, Munich, 1963, and Generalfeldmarschall Wilhelm Ritter von Leeb, *Tagebuchaufzeichnungen und Lagebeurteilungen aus zwei Weltkriegen. Aus dem Nachlass*, ed. Georg Meyer, Stuttgart, 1976 (Beiträge zur Militär- und Kriegsgeschichte, 16).

39   Cf. K.-J. Müller, *Das Heer und Hitler*, pp. 53 ff., 63 ff., 68 ff., 77 ff. In this respect a comparison of General Fritsch's directives on matters concerning the training of the officer corps with the corresponding instructions of the Minister is illuminating: see the sources in *Offiziere im Bild von Dokumenten aus drei Jahrhunderten*, cited in note 10.

40   On this point see the detailed study by K.-J. Müller, *Ludwig Beck*, 1979, chapter III.

41 'Decree on the Provisional Wartime Leadership Structure', printed in *Spiegelbild einer Verschwörung. Die Kaltenbrunner-Berichte an Bormann und Hitler über das Attentat vom 20. Juli 1944. Geheime Dokumente aus dem ehemaligen Reichssicherheitshauptamt*, ed. Archiv Peter, Stuttgart, 1961, pp. 31–3.

42 See the bibliographical references cited in note 24 above and the second chapter of the present volume.

43 See the memoranda worked out in the general staff on the question of the organisation of the military leadership, reproduced in K.-J. Müller, *Das Heer und Hitler*, documents 25–7, and the interpretation in *ibid.*, pp. 211–43, and in K.-J. Müller, *Ludwig Beck*, chapter III.

44 Beck's memorandum of 29 May 1938, printed in K.-J. Müller, *Ludwig Beck*, document No. 46.

45 Accordingly, Beck said to a confidant in November 1938, 'Since May I have only pursued the one thought — How do I avoid a war?' (cf. *ibid.*, document No. 55).

46 B. Scheurig, *Tresckow*, p. 54 ff.

47 *Ibid.*, p. 59 ff.

48 *Ibid.*

49 *Ibid.*, p. 60 ff.

50 *Ibid.*, p. 66 ff.

51 *Ibid.*, pp. 88, 96–119; for an analogous development in the case of Stauffenberg see Christian Müller, *Oberst i. G. Stauffenberg. Eine Biographie*, Düsseldorf, 1970.

52 K.-J. Müller, *Das Heer und Hitler*, document No. 4.

53 See the interpretation in *ibid.*, p. 83 ff. On Manstein's attitude towards the Nazi genocide policy in Russia see Jehuda L. Wallach, 'Feldmarschall Erich von Manstein und die deutsche Judenausrottung in Russland', *Jahrbuch des Instituts für deutsche Geschichte*, IV, 1975, pp. 457–72, and A. Hillgruber, 'In der Sicht des kritischen Historikers', in *Nie ausser Dienst. Zum achtzigsten Geburtstag von Generalfeldmarschall Erich von Manstein*, Cologne, 1967, pp. 77–7.

54 H. Stieff, *Ausgewählte Briefe, loc. cit.* (see note 38).

55 Rudolf Christoph Freiherr von Gersdorff, *Soldat im Untergang*, Frankfurt, Berlin and Vienna, 1977, pp. 86 ff., 112 ff.

56 Gersdorff's memoirs offer impressive examples of this process of development.

57 In this regard the reaction of some officers, already critical of certain developments within the Reich, to the signing of the pact between Hitler and Stalin is typical. For General Beck just as for Major Groscurth and Captain Liedig, both officers in the Intelligence Department, for instance, the anxiety about internal 'radicalisation' of party rule combined with worries about foreign policy. In their eyes Hitler had now, by means of the pact with Bolshevist Russia, synchronised his foreign policy with the supposedly social revolutionary tendencies of the 'radicals' in the Nazi camp. For Beck, in addition to several other references, see K.-J. Müller, *Ludwig Beck*, document No. 55; for Groscurth, *Tagebücher*, p. 25, 69 ff., 509 ff.

The pact evoked relief in other officers who still agreed domestically with the regime but had strong international worries in view of Hitler's policy. See E. Wagner, *Generalquartiermeister*, p. 91; further reactions in K.-J. Müller, *Das Heer und Hitler*, p.414 ff.

58 There is a thorough analysis of this subject in H. C. Deutsch, *The Conspiracy against Hitler*, especially chapters III, VI and VII, and in K.-J. Müller, *Das Heer und Hitler*, chapter XI.

59 On the criticism of the traditional concept of resistance see P. Hüttenberger, 'Vorüberlegungen zum "Widerstandsbegriff"' (see note 6), especially pp. 117, 121.